DATE DUE

TRUMAN CAPOTE

By KENNETH T. REED

Miami University

TWAYNE PUBLISHERS
A DIVISION OF G.K. HALL & CO., BOSTON

Copyright © 1981 by G. K. Hall & Co.

Published in 1981 by Twayne Publishers,
A Division of G. K. Hall & Co.
All Rights Reserved

Printed on permanent/durable acid-free paper and bound
in the United States of America

Library of Congress Cataloging in Publication Data

Reed, Kenneth T
Truman Capote.

(Twayne's United States authors series ; TUSAS 388)
Bibliography: p. 137–42
Includes index.
1.   Capote, Truman 1924–
—Criticism and interpretation.
PS3505.A59Z84   813'.54   80–26056
ISBN 0–8057–7321–5

In Memory of Robert and Patricia Geistert

Contents

About the Author

Kenneth T. Reed completed his undergraduate studies in literature at Miami University (Ohio). In 1961 he received the M. A. degree with emphasis on twentieth century literature from the University of Iowa. He was awarded the Ph.D. degree in American literature at the University of Kentucky in 1968. Since that time he has been a member of the English faculty at Miami University where he holds the rank of Professor.

Dr. Reed has written extensively for scholarly journals on such writers as Harriet Beecher Stowe, Richard Wright, Mark Twain, Stephen Crane, F. Scott Fitzgerald, Emily Dickinson, William Dean Howells, and Washington Irving. His articles, notes, and reviews have been published in *Literature and Psychology, Poe Studies, American Notes & Queries, Studies in Black Literature, The American Transcendental Quarterly*, the *CLA Journal*, and the *Fitzgerald/Hemingway Annual*. His *S. N. Behrman* was published as part of *Twayne's United States Authors Series* in 1975.

Preface

This book is offered as a foreword to a reading of Truman Capote, an immensely talented and intelligent writer about whom much has been commented and relatively little understood. It has been composed with students and their mentors expressly in mind, but also with the intention that it will serve well as a reader's companion for anyone with a curiosity about Capote's literary achievement over a period that now exceeds thirty years. It has also been written upon the assumption that, like any artist of genuine stature and significance, Capote can best be understood through an examination of the bulk of his major work. The late William Faulkner, with whom Capote shares certain literary characteristics, is alleged to have remarked that "the few times I tried to read Truman Capote, I had to give up . . . his literature makes me nervous." For any who share Faulkner's view, the present study may serve to quell an occasional anxiety while at the same time it may provide an occasional insight.

A number of observations about Capote are advanced here, but the primary one provides the rationale for the organization of the book: that Capote's fundamental attitude toward such things as good and evil as well as innocence and experience have remained essentially constant over the years. At the same time, however, his generic inclinations have gradually shifted from the short story to the novel-romance, to what has been called variously "creative reporting" or "reportage." After a largely biographic chapter, the emphasis is upon Capote's management of the short story. The stories themselves have been arranged not only chronologically, but (just as significantly) according to locale. Attention to locale, in turn, sheds some light on his longer fictional narratives, the novel-romances that are treated in Chapter 3: *Other Voices, Other Rooms, The Grass Harp,* and *Breakfast at Tiffany's.* The fourth chapter deals with Capote's successes at the art of reportage, a literary mode that has its origins far back in his development as a writer. Finally, the closing chapter addresses itself to questions of prose style, characterization, theme, and literary influences. While it is true that Capote's literary proclivities toward form and idea are shared with numerous other writers, past and present, there has been no apparent need to explore these relationships at any length. Nor has there been any attempt to relate him in any great detail to the fertile literary traditions of the American South. Finally, the views and opinions expressed here are, as always, subject to disagreement and revision by other devotees of Truman Capote whose critical inclinations may well lead them to still other conclusions about the man and his work.

KENNETH T. REED

Miami University

Acknowledgments

The author wishes to thank Random House, Incorporated, for permission to quote passages from Truman Capote's "A Christmas Memory" which appears in *Breakfast at Tiffany's*, copyright 1958, and from "A Voice from a Cloud" which appears in *The Dogs Bark: Public People and Private Places*, copyright 1973. Thanks also go to Professor Jackson R. Bryer of the University of Maryland for generous permission to reprint sections of his Truman Capote bibliography as it appeared in Irving Malin's *Truman Capote's In Cold Blood: A Critical Handbook*, copyright 1969 by Wadsworth Publishing Company.

Chronology

1924   Truman Capote born September 30 in New Orleans.

1927   Sent to live with relatives in rural Alabama.

1939   Begins submitting short stories to literary quarterlies.

1942   Accepts employment with *The New Yorker.*

1943   Wins an O. Henry Memorial Award for "Miriam."

1948   *Other Voices, Other Rooms.*

1949   *Tree of Night and Other Stories.*

1950   *Local Color.*

1951   *The Grass Harp* (play version staged 1952).

1953   On location in Italy filming his script of *Beat the Devil.*

1954   Musical comedy, *House of Flowers,* on Broadway.

1956   Publishes *The Muses Are Heard* and "A Christmas Memory."

1957   "The Duke in His Domain."

1958   *Breakfast at Tiffany's.*

1960   Begins research for *In Cold Blood.*

1965   *In Cold Blood.*

1966   Wins Mystery Writers of America Edgar Allan Poe Award for *In Cold Blood;* plays host to the "party of the century."

1969   *Trilogy* (film with Frank and Eleanor Perry).

1971   Operated upon for cancer.

1973   *The Dogs Bark.*

1976   Plays Lionel Twain in Neil Simon's film *Murder by Death.*

1979   "Conversational Portraits" in Andy Warhol's *Interview.*

CHAPTER 1

"I Don't Care What Anybody Says About Me As Long As It Isn't True"

L IKE the consummate showman he is, Truman Capote has openly invited attention in recent years from more than one segment of life in America. To the popular, less verbal, nonliterary press and television world, he has quite understandably and unavoidably become a colorful and eccentric object of feature articles and interviews, primarily because of his well-honed, deeply ironic wit and the unfailing and uncanny quickness with which his remarks fly. Gerald Clarke reported in *Esquire* in 1972 that Capote had been "canonized" by television personality Johnny Carson and his wife Suzy as "a Public Character, St. Truman of the Tonight Show."[1] Beyond that distinction, Clarke wrote, "no other American novelist knows so many levels of life so intimately, and no other has observed so closely as has Truman the spoiled monsters that inhabit the rarefied reaches of the very rich." Referring to Capote as "the supreme, ultimate gossip," Clarke said that the novelist "knows, or pretends to know, the sexual habits of nearly everyone."[2] Not all observers of Capote have been amused by his extraliterary life, however. Lis Harris, writing for *The New York Times Book Review* in 1973, commented that "the not particularly endearing public persona of Capote the jet-setter and Capote the let-them-eat-cake arbitor of *le vrai chic* has been allowed to somewhat obscure that of Truman Capote the writer."[3]

But to his more serious literary audience, he has deservedly achieved recognition as one of the more versatile, richly talented, and superbly disciplined American men of letters in the present age. Even so, it appears that his "public" and "literary" reputations will never become altogether unified in our time, simply because the popular impression of Capote as madcap social butterfly and late evening television chatterbox does not appear to square with the penetrating and enlightened vision of life to be found in abundance throughout his short fiction, novels, and excursions into reportage. Some have come to expect artists of Capote's caliber to be reclusive individuals living in at least semisecrecy in quarters known only to a few. And yet Capote's life is as open as the pages of his work. "For thirty years I've lived everywhere and had houses all over the world," he wrote in 1972. "But curiously, no matter where I lived, Spain or Italy or Switzerland, Hong Kong or California, Kansas or London, I always kept an apartment in New York." He continued, "I am a city fellow. I like *pavement*. The sound of my shoes on pavement; stuffed windows; all-night restaurants; sirens in the night— sinister but alive; book and record shops that, on impulse, you can visit at midnight."[4]

In spite of his widespread reputation as one of the more aggressively social of literary figures today, Capote has tailored his life to fit the inclinations and requirements of his own unique personality as a writer. "I like to be alone," he said once. "I like finely made cars, I like lonely motels with their ice machines and eerie anonymity; so sometimes I get behind the wheel and, without warning, without particular destination, drive all alone for as far as a thousand miles. I've only once consulted a psychiatrist; instead, I should have gone for a drive with the top down and a wind blowing and a sun shining."[5] In his private life and in his writing Capote tends to avoid any identification with the "normal" or the "conventional." "What I couldn't survive is the middle ground," he wrote of himself. "The sound of lawn mowers and water sprinklers outside a two-car-garage ranch split-level in Scarsdale or Shaker Heights"[6] has no place in his world.

Although Capote's life is open to public inspection and comment, anyone who attempts to make coherent sense out of the alleged "facts" of his life and upbringing must certainly proceed at his own risk, for what one reads about Capote, even in the ostensibly reliable reference books, is not necessarily so. Certain myths about his early years, especially, are prevalent. Some, indeed, appear to be of his own making. For example, a number of sources presumed to be accurate reveal that around the age of fifteen Capote passed five weeks as a tap dancer on a

Mississippi riverboat. There is also the story that he amused
himself (and made considerable money) painting imaginary
flowers on glass. Another story claimed that he became the
protegé of a well-known fortune teller in the South. Still another
story had it that Capote once earned a living by ghost-writing
speeches for a small-time southern politico. But during a public
televised session with interviewer David Frost, the following
conversation transpired:

Frost: You wanted to be a tap dancer?
    (Laughter)
Capote: Oh, that's just something I put in *Who's Who.*
Frost: It's not true?
Capote: No. You know, they just send you these forms to fill out, what
you wanted to do or be in *Who's Who in America*, and I just sent them
back a sort of a joke thing. I said that I painted on glass and wrote
political speeches and wanted to be a tap dancer, but it was none of it
true.
Frost: Well, how do we know that the other story you just told us is
true?
Capote: Maybe it isn't. (Laughter, applause)[7]

Later in that same interview Capote remarked, "I don't care
what anybody says about me as long as it isn't true."[8]
Consequently, anyone who presumes to reconstruct the facts of
Capote's background is twice warned: he must proceed at his
own peril, trusting neither to published details of the Capote
biographical myth nor to outward appearances and impressions.
Appearance, however, has contributed much of the enduring
public fascination with Capote. *Esquire* interviewer Tom Burke
none-too-kindly described him as being "like a ruined Puck" and
also "like a tiny, blond Theda Bara." He continued, "though
Truman Capote is not a dwarf, nor a hydrocephalic, his head
does appear to have been left under water too long, and his body
seems out of proportion to ordinary surroundings, as if he moved
continually through the room in the fun house where the
furniture is larger than life-size."[9] Other commentators in print
have been scarcely any kinder to Capote. Cynthia Ozick of *The
New Republic* asked, "who is this tiny-fingered flaccid man, with
molasses eyes and eunuch's voice, looking like an old caricature
of Aeolus, the puff-cheeked little god of wind?"[10]

I *Beginnings*

Capote was christened Truman Streckfus Persons at the Touro
Infirmary on September 30, 1924. His mother, then sixteen years
of age, was Nina (Faulk) Persons, a former Miss Alabama who
had married a travelling salesman. "When she was eighteen,"
Capote revealed once in an interview, "she decided that she
wanted to go to college. So I went to college with her, all the way
through, and by the time she was graduated she and my father
were divorced so I went to live with relatives in a rather remote
part of Alabama. This was a very strange household. It consisted
of three elderly ladies and an elderly uncle. They were the
people who had adopted my mother. Her parents had died when
she was very young. I lived there until I was ten, and it was a very
lonely life, and it was then that I became interested in writing."[11]
    Capote grew up an only child in a shattered family. At the time
of his mother's divorce he was four years of age, and it was his
fate to be dispatched from place to place to live. "It was a
complicated divorce with much bitterness on either side, which
is the main reason why I spent most of my childhood wandering
among the homes of relatives in Louisiana, Mississippi, and rural
Alabama," Capote said much later. "Off and on I attended
schools in New York City and Connecticut."[12] One of the persons
who took the young Capote in was Miss Sook Faulk, "a spinster
relative in a rural, remote part of Alabama."[13] He was to
remember her with the greatest affection and to portray her
later in a combination of short fiction and autobiographical
reporting. "She herself was not more than twelve years old
mentally, which is what accounted for her purity, timidity, her
strange, unexpected wisdom. I have written two stories about
her, 'A Christmas Memory,' and 'The Thanksgiving Visitor.'"[14]
Miss Faulk knew young Truman as "Buddy," he wrote in "A
Christmas Memory," associating him with "a boy who was
formerly her best friend. The other Buddy died in the 1880's,
when she was a child." Undoubtedly, the inspiration for much of
Capote's skill as a southern local colorist comes from Miss Faulk
and her immediate surroundings. Capote once recalled a day in
1932 when he was about eight years old and under the custody of
Miss Faulk:

I am in a vegetable garden humming with bees and heat waves, and I am picking and putting into a basket turnips and slushy scarlet tomatoes. Then I am running through a pine and honeysuckle woods toward a deep cool creek, where I bathe and wash the turnips, the tomatoes. Birds, bird-music, leaf-light, the stringent taste of raw turnip on my tongue: pleasures everlasting, hallelujah. Not far away a snake, a cotton-mouth moccasin, writhes, ripples across the water; I'm not afraid of it.[15]

Later he remembered the loving, fruitcake-making Sook Faulk as his true mother surrogate:

. . . my friend Miss Faulk is making a scrap-quilt, the design is of roses and grapes, and now she is drawing the quilt up to my chin. There is a kerosene lamp by the bed; she wishes me happy birthday, and blows out the light.[16]

Notwithstanding, Monroeville, Alabama, did not entirely agree with the young man. "By and large," he told Pati Hill of *The Paris Review*, "my childhood was spent in parts of the country and among people unprovided with any semblance of a cultural attitude."[17] At this point, the authenticity of the biographical record becomes questionable. Inconsistencies begin to indicate the operation of Capote's fertile imagination. Capote reported to Hill that in Monroeville "I was thought somewhat *eccentric,* which was fair enough, and *stupid,* which I suitably resented. Still, I despised school—or schools, for I was always changing from one to another—and year after year failed the simplest subjects out of loathing and boredom. I played hooky at least twice a week and was always running away from home. Once I ran away with a friend who lived across the street—a girl much older than myself who in later life achieved a certain fame. Because she murdered a half-dozen people and was electrocuted at Sing Sing."[18]

Capote continued to spend at least his summers in Alabama until 1939. In 1934, when he was not yet ten, he wrote his first book, a roman à clef which he entitled "Old Mr. Busybody," entering it in a writing contest sponsored by the *Mobile Press Register.* "The first installment apppeared one Sunday . . . only somebody suddenly realized that I was serving up a local scandal

as fiction, and the second installment never appeared. Naturally,
I didn't win a thing," he remembered years later.[19] Soon after
this incident he was sent to live with a family in Pass Christian,
Mississippi, and it was here that both the scene and the situation
for his autobiographic novel *Other Voices, Other Rooms* were
suggested to him; for years later he cast his mind back to scenes
of Pass Christian and dimly recalled having lived in a house with
an asthmatic old man in it who passd his time in a darkened room
smoking medicinal cigarettes and sewing scrap quilts.

Capote has indicated that at about the age of ten he developed
an interest in Willa Cather, Gustave Flaubert, and Marcel
Proust.[20] "Proust may have had the greatest effect on me, more
as a person that as an artist," he revealed to Gloria Steinem in
1967. "I always felt that he was kind of a secret friend."[21] By the
time he was twelve, he said during a television interview with
David Frost, "all the teachers thought that I was much brighter
than I was."[22] And yet in his *Paris Review* conversation, Capote
spoke of his school principal's having called on his guardians to
inform them "that in his opinion, and in the opinion of the
faculty, I was 'subnormal.' He thought it would be sensible, the
humane action, to send me to some special school equipped to
handle backward brats." He continued, "In an effort to prove
that I wasn't subnormal [my guardians] pronto packed me off to
a psychiatric study clinic at a university in the East [Columbia]
where I had my I.Q. inspected. I enjoyed it thoroughly and—
guess what?—came home a genius, so proclaimed by science."[23]

He elaborated more on the testing of his intelligence to
Steinem, explaining that as a Works Progress Administration
project during the Depression a team of psychological research-
ers had been dispatched to rural areas in Alabama to administer
intelligence tests. Having tested Capote twice, they computed a
score that was supposedly the highest they had ever seen. The
team then secured his mother's permission to test again for an
entire week at Columbia University, where they confirmed the
information they had collected in Alabama. The results of the
tests convinced Capote's guardians, he told Steinem, "that I
wasn't stupid, but they still thought I was very odd. They really
hadn't wanted me to come home from New York a genius, just a
nice normal boy. But the experience gave me confidence, and by
the time I was ten, I was sitting up all night long to write. The

excitement was so great that I couldn't relax at all until I discovered whiskey. Then I would take a few swigs before going to bed. Eventually my little hoard of bottles was discovered, and that put an end to that."[24] Capote remained proud of his intelligence quotient, and proclaimed in 1972 that he had "the highest intelligence of any child in the United States, an I.Q. of 215."[25]

By 1939 Capote's mother had gone to New York and had married her second husband, Joseph Garcia Capote, a Cuban businessman who legally adopted his wife's sixteen-year-old son Truman. The young man was then sent for a period of three years to a succession of boarding schools including St. John's [military] Academy and Trinity School, both located in the New York area. He was finally enrolled at Greenwich High School in Millbrook, Connecticut, where he came under the abiding infuence of Catherine Wood. Said Capote much later in life, "the first person who ever really helped me was, strangely, a teacher. An English teacher I had in high school named Catherine Wood, who backed my ambitions in evey way and to whom I shall always be grateful."[26] Professor William Nance indicates that with her encouragement Capote wrote poetry and fiction for the high school paper *(Green Witch)*, and that the 1966 edition of *A Christmas Memory* is dedicated to her.[27] But there is still some question of whether Capote was ever graduated from high school at all. On one occasion he remarked that "I was never a good student, and so intense was my relief when graduation finally came that I did not consider college."[28] On yet two other occasions Capote said that he had not finished his high school studies.[29]

Only recently did Capote reconsider his decision to stay out of college. "I was determined never to set a studious foot inside a college classroom. I felt that either one was or wasn't a writer, and no combination of professors could influence the outcome. I still think I was correct, at least in my own case; however, I now realize that most young writers have more to gain than not by attending college, if only because their teachers and classroom comrades provide a captive audience for their work; nothing is lonelier than to be an aspiring artist without some semblance of a sounding board."[30] In his estimation, the reading he did on his own—especially in Dickens and Twain—was of much greater value than what he referred to as his "official education" which, he said, "was a waste and ended when I was seventeen."[31]

II The New Yorker

Once out of high school, the seventeen-year-old aspiring writer applied for a job with *The New Yorker*, and in this instance also there are contradictions in the biographical record. Rochelle Girson reported in 1949 that Capote had been hired as an assistant accountant, but that he confessed the day after his hiring that he was unable to subtract figures. He was then allegedly transferred to the magazine's art department and put to work unwrapping packages while at the same time he was offering "ideas" to writers of "The Talk of the Town" column, choosing anecdotes for a digest magazine, and reading film scripts.[32]

When questioned about his early dealings with *The New Yorker*, Capote gave a somewhat different version. "Originally," he said, "I was to work for *The New Yorker* in 'The Talk of the Town' department. This was during the war, and I had been sending them stories and articles, and I went to see the people I had been corresponding with; they were going to give me a job. It was during the war and they had lost all their staff. Well, I arrived, and they took one look—I was seventeen and looked about ten years old—and realized they could never send this child labor case out to interview anybody, so in the end I worked in the art department and turned out ideas for 'Talk of the Town' every week and suggested personalities for 'Profiles.' " But the contradiction does not end here. Capote is quoted elsewhere as saying that "I went round to *The New Yorker* magazine and left with a glorious sounding job in their Art Department; in actuality I turned out to be a kind of errand boy."[33]

At the very least, Capote's association with *The New Yorker* introduced him to the world of writers and publishers. One of his haunts was the New York Society Library where he was sent on research assignment and where, he said, "three or four times I noticed this absolutely *marvelous*-looking woman . . . Her suits were soft, but rather severe—very distinguished looking." He later met the mysterious lady under a canopy during a rainstorm, and she invited him to hot chocolate at Longchamps. "She asked me what writers I liked. I told her my very favorite was Willa

Cather. 'That's very interesting,' she said, 'Why?' So I told her why, and we talked for a while. 'Well,' she said finally, 'I'm Willa Cather.'" The interlude overwhelmed him. "When I finally got out into the street again, I was so bowled over that I walked right out into a lamppost."[34]

His employment at *The New Yorker* ended abruptly after two years, for reasons never clearly established. The most colorful version is that in 1943 Capote had "unintentionally but injudiciously [offended] Robert Frost."[35] According to an account in *Esquire*, "Truman had gone to Vermont on vacation, staying at an inn where Frost was giving a reading. Ill with the flu, Truman kept to his room, venturing down to the reading only on the pleadings of the manager, who had heard that he was from *The New Yorker*. Capote was sicker than he thought, however, and soon left. A copy of Frost's poems, thrown by the outraged author himself, sailed after him. 'Who the hell is this Truman Capote, anyway,' asked *New Yorker* editor Harold Ross the next day. Truman went back to Alabama to write *Other Voices, Other Rooms*. He still remembers Frost as 'the meanest man who ever drew breath, an old fake dragging around with a shaggy head of hair and followed by pathetic old ladies from the Middle West.'"[36] In a recent self-interview Capote said that if he were ever to be given "such a degrading assignment" as to be commissioned for an "unforgettable character" article for the *Reader's Digest,* he would write about "Robert Frost, America's Poet Laureate . . . an old bastard if there ever was one."[37] For it was Frost, Capote said, who wrote "a scurrilous letter to Harold Ross" which resulted in Capote's being "fired from [his] first and last clock time job."[38]

III   *Emerging Man of Letters*

From one point of view, Frost's strongly worded letter of complaint to Harold Ross was one of the truly fortunate turns in the literary career of Truman Capote, for while working for the magazine Capote was making only limited progress; in those two years of employment he sold a few short stories to "little" magazines, although on one occasion when he was still seventeen he received three literary acceptances in the same day's mail. He unsuccessfully attempted several times to have fiction published in *The New Yorker;* one story was returned with the comment,

"Very good. But romantic in a way this magazine is not." Shortly before his departure from *The New Yorker* Capote was at work on a novel he entitled *Summer Crossing* for which he never sought a publisher. "It was in order to complete the book that I took courage, quit [?] my job, left New York and settled with relatives, a cotton-growing family who lived in a remote part of Alabama," he wrote in 1969. And it was at this point in his life that he began successfully to place his fiction "with some regularity in a number of magazines."[39] The stories he wrote in Alabama were ultimately to be among his best: "Miriam," "Shut a Final Door," and "A Tree of Night."

In Alabama in 1943 Capote began what was to be by all odds the best of his longer fiction. This was *Other Voices, Other Rooms*. He described the genesis of that book in an essay called "A Voice from a Cloud" that he used as introduction to the twentieth anniversary edition of the novel. A substantial portion of the essay follows:

It was early winter when I arrived there, and the atmosphere of the roomy farmhouse, entirely heated by stoves and fireplaces, was well suited to a fledgling novelist wanting quiet isolation. The household rose at four-thirty, breakfasted by electric light, and was off about its business as the sun ascended—leaving me home alone and, increasingly, in a panic. For, more and more, *Summer Crossing* seemed to me too thin, clever, unfelt. Another language, a secret spiritual geography, was burgeoning inside me, taking hold of my night-dream hours as well as my wakeful daydreams. One frosty December afternoon I was far from home, walking in a forest along the bank of a mysterious, deep, very clear creek, a route that led eventually to a place called Hatter's Mill. The mill, which straddled the creek, had been abandoned long ago; it was a place where farmers had brought their corn to be ground into cornmeal. As a child, I'd often gone there with cousins to fish and swim; it was while exploring under the mill that I'd been bitten in the knee by a cotton-mouth moccasin—precisely as happens to Joel Knox [the protagonist in *Other Voices, Other Rooms*]. And now as I came upon the forlorn mill with its sagging silver-gray timbers, the remembered shock of the snakebite returned; and other memories too—of Idabel, or rather the girl who was the counterpart of Idabel, and how we used to wade and swim in the pure waters, where fat speckled fish lolled in sunlit pools; Idabel was always trying to reach out and grab one.

Excitement—a variety of creative coma—overcame me. Walking home, I lost my way and moved in circles round the woods, for my mind was reeling with the whole book. . . .

It was dark when I got home, and cold, but I didn't feel the cold because of the fire inside me. . . . I said good night, locked myself in my room, tossed the manuscript of *Summer Crossing* into a bottom bureau drawer, collected several sharp pencils and a fresh pad of yellow lined paper, got into bed fully clothed, and with pathetic optimism, wrote: "*Other Voices, Other Rooms*—a novel by Truman Capote." Then: "Now a traveller must make his way to Noon City by the best means he can. . . ."

Capote labored over the novel for the next three years, eventually moving himself and his projects to New Orleans. "I thanked my exasperated relatives for their generosity, their burdened patience, and bought a ticket on a Greyhound bus to New Orleans," he recorded in "A Voice from a Cloud." It was here that he rented a bedroom from a Creole family on Royal Street in the French Quarter. "New Orleans was my hometown and I had many friends there," he now recalls, ". . . but I never saw a soul I knew. Except by accident, my father. Which was ironic considering that though I was unaware of it at the time, the central theme of *Other Voices, Other Rooms* was my search for the existence of this essentially imaginary person."[40] From here, Capote moved to Nantucket Island where he completed the book.

In the meantime Capote had enjoyed successes that indicated that he would more than survive as a writer. In 1943 he won the O. Henry Memorial Award for "Miriam," and published "The Walls are Cold" in the fourth quarter edition of *Decade of Short Stories.* In the following year the same magazine printed "A Mink of One's Own" and "The Shape of Things" in the third and fourth quarter issues respectively. The May, 1945 issue of *Story* carried "My Side of the Matter," and that winter the *Prairie Schooner* ran his latest story, "Preacher's Legend." In 1946, "Shut a Final Door" was selected for inclusion in the O. Henry Memorial Award volume of short fiction. Also in 1946 Capote attracted the attention of Random House and signed a contract, including a $1,500 advance, for his novel in progress, *Other Voices, Other Rooms.*[41] Now having reached the age of twenty-three, he tried his hand as a critic and wrote a review of the 1946 New York theater season which he titled "This Winter's Mask" for the December issue of *Harper's Bazaar.*

When Random House brought out *Other Voices, Other Rooms* in 1948 replete with a now famous, vaguely suggestive photograph of Capote supine on a divan, national literary attention turned his way. The photograph, in the words of Cynthia Ozick, depicted Capote "languid but sovereign, lolling in the turn of a curved sofa in a bow tie and tattersall vest, with tender mouth and such strange, elf-cold eyes."[42] Capote was clearly unhappy about the picture and about the way the book was received: "There were many cruel things written about me at the time," he recalled later, "and a great deal of comment about the photograph on the back of the book (which was perfectly innocent). Somehow, all the publicity I read about it in the newspapers . . . well, I wasn't used to reading about myself. I was so shocked and hurt that I never got any pleasure out of it at all." He continued, "since I didn't get that satisfaction from it—in fact I got the exact opposite—it just sobered me up a great deal and made me realize on what paths I truly must go."[43]

The reviews of *Other Voices, Other Rooms* to which Capote referred were volatile, if nothing else. J. E. Cross of *The Library Journal* found it to be "much lush writing, frequently trailing off into illusory fancies of sick brains, losing its way, yet withal picturesque. Not recommended for libraries." In *The New York Times* Carlos Baker wrote that "the story of Joel Knox did not need to be told, except to get it out of the author's system." "The distasteful trappings of its homosexual theme overhang it like Spanish moss," said *Time*. C. J. Rollo of *The Atlantic Monthly* found the novel "intense, brilliant, and—as a novel—a half failure: too formless and too choked with gaudy blossoms." Capote reacted to these and other such reviews by embarking on a tour of Haiti and France.

He continued to travel and to write. *Tree of Night and Other Stories* was published by Random House in February of 1949. He contributed "Faulkner Dances," a critique of the choreographed novel *As I Lay Dying,* to the April, 1949 issue of *Theatre Arts.*

In the meantime, Random House encouraged Capote's literary popularity by issuing more of his writing at yearly intervals (*Local Color* in 1950, *The Grass Harp* in 1951), while Capote remained in, and wrote about, his villa ("A House in Sicily," *Harper's Bazaar,* January, 1951).

III   Stage and Film

Early in 1952, *The Grass Harp,* a play based upon his novel published that same year, was in rehearsal for its Broadway opening. "Playwriting has little to do with literary talent," Capote told Harvey Breit of *The New York Times*. "The theatre is so extraordinarily visual, and in order to write for it I had to forget the novel. It's as though someone asked you to take a painting and make a statue of it. It's impossible. You can make the statue carry the same feeling and motivation as the painting, but it's a totally different thing. I actually looked at the book twice."[44] The play was produced at the Martin Beck Theater on March 27, but closed after an unsuccessful run.

For the time being, Capote had become interested in writing for stage and cinema. In Ravello, Italy in 1952 he was on location with a comic adventure film script for Humphrey Bogart and director John Huston, called *Beat the Devil*. Capote's writing was so poor, in Huston's estimation, that he "simply couldn't stomach [it] once he actually read it."[45] To rectify certain problems in the script, Capote not infrequently rewrote by night, and handed the actors their parts the following morning. After the viewing of the finished product, Bogart allegedly told Capote that he would never forgive him, ironically, for in the opinion of Michael Kernan of *The Washington Post*, the picture was one of Bogart's best.[46] Huston was no happier about the picture than was Bogart. "Every time someone mentions it to Huston," Capote said to Kernan, "he shifts his eyes and mumbles something about how it was Capote's film."[47] Capote made himself more unpopular with Huston when, having won $150.00 by defeating Bogart at Indian hand wrestling, he boasted that he "could put [Bogart] right on [his] bottom like that."[48] He succeeded, but in the course of wrestling did injury to Bogart's elbow, putting him out of the picture for three days. Huston blamed Capote for having added twenty thousand dollars to the cost of the film by disabling the leading man.[49] *Beat the Devil* was finally released by United Artists in 1954.

After his mother's suicide in 1953, Capote wrote another Broadway extravaganza, a flashy musical entitled *House of Flowers*, based upon his short story. The play opened at the Alvin Theatre on December 30, 1954, but like *The Grass Harp* before it, soon closed. Apparently dissatisfied with his theatrical experiments, Capote turned again to prose writing. Associated once more with *The New Yorker* in 1955, he travelled on assignment for that magazine to Russia with the American cast of *Porgy and Bess*. In *The Muses Are Heard* (1956), he reported on

his adventures behind the Iron Curtain in the company of an
"enormous troupe, consisting of fifty-eight actors, seven back-
stage personnel, two conductors, assorted wives and office
workers, six children and their schoolteacher, three journalists,
two dogs and one psychiatrist."[50]

His interest in reportage whetted, Capote demonstrated his
immense skill at creative autobiography in his childhood
recollection "A Christmas Memory" which appeared in the
December, 1956 issue of *Mademoiselle*. Favorable reception to
this led Capote to additional experimentation. "What," he once
asked himself, "is the most banal thing in journalism? . . . I
realized it would be an interview with a film star, the sort of
thing you would see in *Photoplay* magazine. . . . So I put a
number of names into a hat and pulled out, God knows why,
Marlon Brando. He was in Japan . . . so I went to *The New Yorker*
and asked them if they'd be interested in this, and they
were. . . . I had dinner with [Brando] and then spent a year on
the piece because it had to be perfection—because my part was
to take this banal thing and turn it into a work of art."[51] The final
product of this unique assignment in biography was "The Duke
in His Domain" which *The New Yorker* printed in 1957. Some
fifteen years after the extensive Brando interviews, Capote's
original fascination with the actor had sobered somewhat. "No
actor of my generation," he said, "possesses greater natural gifts;
but none other has transported intellectual falsity to higher
levels of hilarious pretension. Except, perhaps, Bob Dylan."[52]

IV *A Second Career*

"My second career began . . . with *Breakfast at Tiffany's,*"
Capote said once.[53] "I think I've had two careers. One was a
career of precocity, the young person who published a number of
books that were really quite remarkable. I can't read them now,
and evaluate them favorably, as though they were the work of a
stranger."[54] He recently commented more on his "first" career:
"I am not a keen rereader of my own books: what's done is done.
Moreover, I am always afraid of finding that my harsher
detractors are correct and that the work is not as good as I
choose to think it."[55] Speaking pointedly of *Other Voices, Other
Rooms*, he commented, "I was startled by its symbolic subter-
fuges. Also, while there are passages that seem to me accom-
plishments, others arouse uneasiness. On the whole, though, it

was as if I were reading the fresh-minted manuscript of a total
stranger. I was impressed by him. For what he had done has the
enigmatic shine of a strangely colored prism held to the light—
that, and a certain anguished, pleading intensity like the message
of a ship-wrecked sailor stuffed into a bottle and thrown into the
sea."[56]

With *Breakfast at Tiffany's*, Capote set out in a new direction.
This was an engaging short novel concerning an irrepressible
young New Yorker named Holiday "Holly" Golightly; Capote
had moved his setting away from the South, and had largely
abandoned the gothic solemnity of *Other Voices, Other Rooms*
and a goodly number of his better short stories. Published in
1958, *Breakfast at Tiffany's* contributed to the evidence that
won Capote a creative writing award from the National Institute
of Arts and Letters the following year.

Between November, 1959 and April, 1965, Truman Capote's
energies were devoted almost exclusively to the western Kansas
murder of the Herbert Clutter family by Perry Smith and
Richard Hickock. During that six-year period when he collected
and assimilated enough notes to fill a small room and then sifted
through them for the writing of *In Cold Blood*, he also developed
a dependency upon tranquilizers. If the writing of his book had
not been enough of an emotional strain, his emotional relationship with the killers themselves made that interlude in his life all
but psychologically debilitating.

At the time of his initial interest in the case he had only
recently completed a series of biographic commentaries for
Richard Avedon's book of photographs entitled *Observations*
(1959), and was living in Brooklyn Heights. Even with his nearly
total immersion in the horrid circumstances of the Clutter
tragedy, he collaborated with William Archebald on a 1961
screen version of Henry James's *The Turn of the Screw* which
they titled *The Innocents*. It became a Twentieth Century-Fox
film, starring Deborah Kerr and Michael Redgrave. The film
version of *Breakfast at Tiffany's* (Paramount) also appeared in
1961, with Audrey Hepburn, George Peppard, and Patricia Neal.
In 1963 Capote published a review of Michel Brown's *Mobile* in
The New York Review of Books, and in April of the following year
he contributed a travel article ("Plisetskaya: 'A Two-Headed
Calf'") to *Vogue*. For the June, 1965 issue of *Redbook* he produced a piece called "A Curious Gift."

Capote was in London in July of 1965, the house guest of

Ambassador and Mrs. David K. E. Bruce. Another of the guests was sixty-five-year-old Adlai Stevenson, twice defeated for the presidency, but currently the United States representative at the United Nations. "I've known a few politicians whom I liked," Capote said once. "Adlai Stevenson was a friend, and always a generous one."[57] On the afternoon of July 14, three months to the day after the deaths of Smith and Hickock, Stevenson collapsed and died some fifty yards from the embassy, after efforts to resuscitate him failed. On the previous evening Capote had complimented Stevenson on his necktie. Stevenson promised to make him a gift of it. After Stevenson's death, Capote said, "I remember watching a manservant pack his belongings, and then when the suitcases were so pathetically filled, but still unclosed, I walked in and helped myself [to the necktie]—a sort of sentimental theft. . . ."[58]

Death, although it plays a major role in Capote's consciousness and in his writing, is no more a preoccupation with him than it is with such other major American writers as Edgar Allan Poe or William Faulkner. "It strikes me as absurd and rather obscene, this whole cosmetic and medical industry based on a lust for youth, age-fear, death terror. Who the hell wants to live forever? Most of us, apparently, but it's idiotic. After all, there *is* such a thing as life-saturation: the point when everything is pure effort and total repetition."[59] Capote himself narrowly escaped death in a 1969 automobile accident in Southampton, New York, when he was, in his own words, "flung thrugh the windshield head-on, and though seriously wounded and certain that what Henry James called The Distinguished Thing (death) was nearby, lay fully conscious in pools of blood reciting . . . the telephone numbers of various friends." Then in 1971 he was operated upon for cancer, about which he commented that "the only altogether upsetting part was that I had to loiter around an aimless week between the day of diagnosis and the morning of the knives."[60]

Fortunately, not everything went awry in 1965 and after; for it was in that year that *In Cold Blood* (upon which he had worked since 1959) not only appeared, but except for a few inevitable detractors, was acclaimed by most critics as a book of immense distinction. The research and writing that had gone into it, however, had taken a devastating emotional toll on its author. "I used to have a chart on the board of people I'd written to, things to be done, people who have answered, people who haven't answered—the most minute little details—I would never do it again. I mean, if I had known what that book was going to cost in every conceivable way, emotionally, I never would have started it, and I really mean that," he said just after the book appeared.[61] It was at this time, however, that Capote was honored by the Mystery Writers of America Edgar Allan Poe Award. Further more, the 1966-1968 period in his career was one of the more productive. In January of 1966 he published "The 'Sylvia' Odyssey" in *Vogue*, and the following month the same magazine carried his "Two Faces . . . A Landscape." In December, "Truman Capote Introduces Jane Bowles" appeared in *Mademoiselle*. He contributed a piece called "Oliver Smith" to Roddy McDowell's *Double Exposure* (1966), while later that year Random House printed a special edition of *A Christmas Memory*. Also in 1966 the Providence Trinity Square Repertory Company produced a musical version of *The Grass Harp*.

Capote's short story "Among the Paths to Eden" was aired as a television play in 1967, the same year that Richard Brooks's screen version of *In Cold Blood* was released by Columbia Pictures. *Vogue* published one of Capote's travel pieces ("'Extreme Magic'—An Awake Dream, Cruising Up the Yugoslavian Coast") in April of 1967. On Thanksgiving Day that year, television audiences were treated to an adaptation of "The Thanksgiving Visitor," while on the following January 28 a rewritten version of the ill-fated *House of Flowers* opened at the Theatre de Lys and eventually closed after fifty-seven performances.

V   *The Party of the Decade*

Because the reputation of Capote the public personality is inextricably twined with that of Capote the literary man, there can be no omission of what, in 1966, some New Yorkers referred to as The Party of the Decade. To his popular, mostly nonliterary audience, the moment of Capote's greatness arrived early in December of that year when, after some of the strain of writing *In Cold Blood* had eased, he celebrated by entertaining some five hundred of "just [his] real friends" in the ballroom at New York's Hotel Plaza. "It was the party of the century, or plainly it was the biggest and most glorious bash ever," *Life* reported.

Capote's "friends [were] as lustrous, most of them, as they were whimsically diverse . . . Princess Peggy d'Arenberg . . . jetted in from Paris, and Alvin Dewey, the detective hero of Capote's *In Cold Blood*, came from Garden City, Kansas . . . There was a pop artist or two, Nicholas de B. Katzenbach and more Fords than would fit under the hood of a Lincoln Continental. The mother of John F. Kennedy came, as did the daughter of Theodore Roosevelt, the daughter of Harry S. Truman, and Lynda Bird Johnson. Possibly any number of people could have brought together the rich, the talented, the top hats, the cloth caps, the hip set, the pop set and the cop set under one roof. But no one but Truman Capote could have made them love it."[62]

The party, indeed, included some of the more illustrious names and unlikely combinations of personalities imaginable. Present were Andy Warhol, Walter Lippmann, William Buckley, Arthur Schlesinger, Norman Mailer, Marianne Moore, guest of honor Kay Graham, Sargent and Eunice Shriver, Philip Roth, George Plimpton, Princess Radziwill, Tallulah Bankhead, Mrs. Henry Ford II, Ralph Ellison, all of them appropriately masked for the ball. Said the host in his thirty-nine-cent mask from F.A.O. Schwarz: "I really don't think anyone else could have done it— could have brought all these people together— because nobody knows them all."[63] Capote explained to one reporter covering the event that "the whole point of a bal masqué is to ask anyone you want to dance and sit wherever you want, and then when the mask comes off at midnight, you can find out who your new chums are, or join your old chums."[64] The scene at the Plaza ended at around four in the morning when Peter Duchin's orchestra struck up "Good Night Ladies."

After The Party of the Decade, Capote became, perhaps, a little less visible. A year from his October, 1969 automobile accident in Southampton, New York, a judge in Santa Ana, California, found the writer guilty of contempt of court when he failed to appear as a witness in the murder trial of a person he had been interviewing. Capote was sentenced to three days in the Orange County Jail, but was released through the efforts of a physician and an attorney. *The New York Times* reported that on October 22 "the author, stubble-bearded and looking tired, was released today from jail, a day after his doctor said that he was worried about Mr. Capote's health."[65]

Since 1969, Capote has had at least two books in progress. The first is an apparently ambitious and lengthy novel called *Answered Prayers*. The novel, he said, "is about four people who got exactly what they set out to get in life. The title comes from something St. Theresa is supposed to have said: 'More tears are shed over answered prayers than unanswered ones.' "[66] Furthermore, he commented much later, "The book has in it any sort of person I've ever had any dealings with."[67] In 1972, supposedly, only one of the editors at Random House had read what Capote had accomplished on the novel, and he remarked that what he had seen of *Answered Prayers* was "brilliant, malicious, very funny, acerbic, bitchy, and unputdownable."[68]

The second of his projects said to be in progress is another excursion into reportage, this one a treatment of the 1973 sex-related murders of at least twenty-seven young men around Houston, Texas, by eighteen-year-old Elmer Henley, Jr. Capote told *The Washington Post* in January, 1974, "I see the trial as a jumping-off point to really tell about this whole extraordinary culture—in Texas and the Southwest, all the way to California—of aimless wandering, this mobile, uprooted life: the seven-mile-long trailer parks, the motorcycles, the campers, the people who have no addresses or even last names."[69]

That Capote should take a vital interest in life's wanderers is not difficult to see, for the writer himself is a wanderer, but with more than one exotic address. The last known of these was Switzerland, about which Capote said, "I have a Chalet . . . high up in the Alps. And I spend every Christmas there . . . everything is in deep snow. And there's this marvelous silvery jingly thing about it. A kind of quiet. Big wood burning fires. A coziness about it that I like, a great sort of purity. It seems to be in the spirit of everything.[70]

CHAPTER 2

Short Fiction:
The Ten Dollar Dream

CAPOTE remarked once to an interviewer that his "more unswerving ambitions still revolve around" the complex art of the short story. "When seriously explored," he continued, "the short story seems to me the most difficult and disciplining form of prose writing extant. Whatever control and technique I have," he said, "I owe entirely to my training in this medium."[1] The expression "my training" should be borne in mind especially, for in a general way, Capote began as a writer of short fiction before turning his attention to the novel-romance. Finally, except for a foray or two into the theater, he developed the craft of reportage which became the artistic mainstay of his more recent years. Still, the great bulk of his short fiction was written in the 1940s, beginning most notably with "A Tree of Night" which was published originally in 1943. The more recent of his shorter fiction, however, is the chronologically isolated "Mojave" which appeared in 1975.

An examination of the tales in order of chronology, however, does not altogether illuminate the intriguing diversity of the shorter pieces. Much depends on Capote's keen sense of place, and the diversity of his short stories is compounded by his tendency to select either the rural South or metropolitan New York as the locality-setting for most of his work. Undoubtedly, the kinds of characters that appear, as well as the particular kinds of dilemmas in which they find themselves, are closely related either to the urbanized impersonality of city life, or to the hidebound agrarian personality of the southern mode of life as it is lived mostly in Louisiana and Alabama. It is impossible that the southern tales could have been rewritten with New York as the setting, nor could his citified stories been adapted to the isolated backlands of rural Alabama.

34

I *Tales of New York*

Eight of the stories, namely "The Walls Are Cold" (1943), "A Mink of One's Own" (1944), "Miriam" (1945), "The Headless Hawk" (1946), "Shut a Final Door" (1947), "Master Misery" (1949), "Among the Paths to Eden" (1960), and (to a limited extent) "Mojave" (1975), are tales of New York. In general, the care and the subsequent artistic quality with which the pieces were written, tended to improve, predictably enough, with Capote's growth as a writer. The stories gradually become richer both in linguistic skill as well as in dark thematic implications—so much so, in fact, that the earlier tales show surprisingly little stylistic resemblance to the later ones.

For example, "The Walls Are Cold" is perhaps closer to a vignette than to one of Capote's later and far more finished short stories. The scene is set in one of the upper floors of a relatively plush city apartment building where a drinking party, presided over by a fickle sixteen-year-old girl named Louise, is well in progress. The hour is two o'clock in the morning, and among the guests is a group of sailors, all of them strangers to Louise. She singles out one of them, a Mississippian known only as Jake, and proceeds to tease him with a succession of sexual overtures, eventually inviting him into the confines of her bedroom where the walls are done in a "cold green." When, after some hesitation, he accepts her invitation to kiss, he also moves his hand against her breasts. She reacts by giving him a "violent shove" that sends him "sprawling across the cold, green rug," and he in turn reacts by vacating the premises. Louise then resolves to sleep that night in the security of her mother's bedroom where "the walls were pale rose and warm."

There are contrasting elements in this brief narrative that give it some slight significance. The first of these is Louise herself, a spoiled and indulged citified adolescent girl living in the midst of fairly opulent circumstances, and Jake, a hapless and far less privileged young person, eight months into a wartime interlude with the Navy. Another of the contrasts is the more pastoral life Jake had known back in Mississippi versus the life he sees at the party: "I never saw anything like it," he exclaims as she ushers him around her apartment. Still another contrast is the change that the girl's adolescent temperament undergoes, a jolting shift from being coyly seductive to outrightly belligerent within the space of a few minutes.

But the story, such as it is, belongs to Louise, whose lack of empathy toward others such as Jake, who are actively involved in the waging of a war, prefigures the otherwise nameless "white pompadoured woman" in "The Shape of Things" which was published a year later. Otherwise, Louise is like the walls of her bedroom: both cold and green. Jake, on the other hand, is at least partially initiated into some of life's more unpleasant realities, and perhaps as a result of this he lives a less self-absorbed, narcissistic way of life. He is forced to accept, after all, the regimentation of military existence in spite of his aversion to it: "I don't take to this kind of life, I don't like others bossin' me around."

"The Walls Are Cold" shares with "A Mink of One's Own" a certain vague consciousness that somewhere in the distance there is indeed a war being waged, except that in "A Mink of One's Own" Capote chose to intensify the elements of irony and deception. Set in New York, it is a wartime story centering upon Mrs. Bertha Munson, a vaguely discontented middle-aged woman who, as the story opens, nervously anticipates brightening one of her otherwise dreary afternoons with a visit from a younger woman named Vini Rondo who has supposedly lived a far more colorful, and altogether more privileged, existence than Mrs. Munson ever had. Vini, an American living in Paris until the German occupation, has (according to newspaper gossip columns) been married to "some Count or Baron or something."

The story's irony becomes evident when Vini Rondo arrives at Mrs. Munson's apartment door on this January afternoon with her hair uncombed, her teeth unbrushed, her nails revealing chipped enamel, her fingers "jewel-less," and her body clothed only in a summer print dress. She carries a large pink box containing a mink coat and says that she wants Mrs. Munson to have it, meaning that she expects Mrs. Munson to offer her money for it. ("I feel I should get something back on my investment," she says.) Distinctly ill at ease, Mrs. Munson tenders an offer of $400.00 which she evidently cannot afford, judging from her standard of living. She writes Vini Rondo a check, primarily, no doubt, to terminate the strained and difficult conversation between them. But once Vini has accepted the check and departed, Mrs. Munson gives the coat "a little yank" and is "terrified to hear the sound of ripping." The coat has disintegrated.

The chief deception in the story is evident at this moment when Mrs. Munson realizes that the coat is literally rotten and therefore worthless. Too late to rectify the situation, she realizes also that "Vini wouldn't phone tomorrow or ever again," and that she must somehow justify the expenditure to her husband, admitting that she has "been taken and taken good." And yet it is not Vini who provides all of the story's deceptions, for when she alleges that for the past year she has been living in California, Mrs. Munson replies, "Oh California, I love California!" even though "she had never been farther west than Chicago."

"A Mink of One's Own" is not a memorable piece of fiction from any point of view, although there are signs to be found in it that point the direction that Capote's writing was about to take. Vini Rondo herself is the forerunner of certain other emotionally disturbed, urbanized young women characters, expecially Miriam (in the story of the same name), D. J. in "The Headless Hawk," Sylvia in "Master Misery," and Holly Golightly in *Breakfast at Tiffany's*. As an easily intimidated New York apartment dweller, Mrs. Munson bears an obvious similarity to the neurotic Mrs. Miller in "Miriam." Furthermore, the deceptions used against these women are fairly typical of Capote's use of deceptions in his 1943 story "A Tree of Night" as well as in a good deal of the fiction he had yet to write, especially "Preacher's Legend," "The Headless Hawk," "Shut a Final Door," "Children on Their Birthdays," "Master Misery," "Jug of Silver," "House of Flowers," "Among the Paths to Eden," *The Thanksgiving Visitor*, and the more ambitious *Other Voices, Other Rooms, The Grass Harp,* and *Breakfast at Tiffany's*.

"Miriam" is a far better story than either "The Walls Are Cold" or "A Mink of One's Own" primarily because of its growing and sustained dramatic intensity and because of its improved handling of psychological crisis. Capote himself evidently cared little for it. "I like . . . several of my short stories," he revealed once during an interview with *The Paris Review*, "though not 'Miriam,' which was a good stunt but nothing more."[2] "Miriam" is, in fact, a kind of tour-de-force, but perhaps no more so than several of the other stories published by that time, especially "A Tree of Night." His lack of enthusiasm for it was apparently a question of personal taste.

"Miriam" has to do with the progressive emotional disintegration of a sixty-one-year-old woman named Mrs. H. T. (Miriam)

Miller, a widow who, until the story opens, had led a comfortably
conservative private existence in a remodeled brownstone close
to New York's East River. Her sedate life and habits are
interrupted, however, by the appearance of a child, also named
Miriam, whom the woman encounters for the first time on a cold
and snowy night while they both queue up for tickets to a movie
house. From this point on the child subtly torments Mrs. Miller
by making personal visits at unlikely hours of the night, and by
moving, bag and baggage, into Mrs. Miller's two rooms with
kitchenette. Mrs. Miller's response to this outlandish series of
events is first puzzlement, then outrage, and finally desperation
to escape the veiled threat to her sanity that Miriam has come to
represent. Mrs. Miller gradually loses her composure, as indicated by her inability to keep track of the days as they pass, and
then by her inhaling from the wrong end of a cork-tipped
cigarette. Driven to desperation, Mrs. Miller eventually runs
down the hallway outside of her apartment and down one
landing, where she attempts to seek help from another tenant in
dealing with her child-intruder, who by this time has provoked
her into genuine fear. When the tenant returns with Mrs. Miller,
however, there is no sign of the child. Only when Mrs. Miller
comes back by herself to her apartment is the girl once again in
evidence. "In times of terror or immense distress," Capote
writes, "there are moments when the mind waits, as though for a
revelation, while a skein of calm is woven over thought; it is like
a sleep, or a supernatural trance." When last seen, the woman
"stiffens" to Miriam's "dull, direct stare."

"Miriam" contains the not unusual pattern in Capote's writing
of the victim and the victimizer, wherein the victim's will is
besieged until it finally weakens and collapses into submission.
Mrs. Miller is a likely victim, however, since she obviously has
not far to travel before she is forced over the line that divides
rationality from despondency. She is also easily threatened and
intimidated, as in the scene where the child takes possession of
the cameo Mrs. Miller's late husband had given her. Like Mrs.
Bertha Munson in "A Mink of One's Own," Mrs. Miller is an
inconspicuous, plain woman living in a state of isolation in the
midst of a huge, densely populated, and largely indifferent city
where she is an ideal target for petty tyranny. In both of these
stories the main characters are threatened by females different
in both age and temperament. Moreover, and this is quite

significant in the development of Capote's fiction, Mrs. Miller chances at one point to come upon a version of the "wizard man," a threatening and recurring male figure in Capote's consciousness; for on the corner of Third Avenue she becomes aware of "an old man, bowlegged and stooped under an armload of bulging packages" who gives her a sinister smile. And although she walks some five blocks, she continues to be aware of "the steady crunch of his footfalls" in the city snow. There is the vague suggestion that he is the same man with whom the child Miriam had last lived, for she has said that "he was terribly poor and we never had good things to eat."

Capote was rather clearly concerned with the question of identity when he wrote "Miriam," for at the end of the story Mrs. Miller is not altogether certain whether she ever did, indeed, "really [know] a girl named Miriam," or whether the encounter she supposedly had with the child was some kind of trick of her own imagination. "For the only thing she had lost to Miriam was her identity," and until the story's final two lines, she believes that she has recovered that illusive identity once more. The question therefore arises whether the child is the alter-ego of the woman, and as in Nathaniel Hawthorne's celebrated short story "Young Goodman Brown," the reader can scarcely distinguish between the dream and the reality of what he has witnessed. Besides the name that the two protagonists share, there is the remark, made on the story's second page, that the child is "lacking [in] any childlike quality whatsoever." But whether literally or figuratively, the child is an expression of the emotional dislocation that lurks just beneath the neat and orderly surface of the upper middle class world of Mrs. Miller.

Perhaps the least interesting of the New York group of stories is "The Headless Hawk" which, because of its structural diffuseness and consequent lack of artistic unity, makes it less compelling than a number of Capote's other pieces. The center of the narrative belongs not, as it would first appear, to a thoroughly perverse runaway from a mental asylum, a girl known only as "D. J.," but to the New York picture gallery manager, Vincent Waters; for it is he, and not the seventeen-year-old girl, who is alluded to in the story's preface from *Job* as one of "those that rebel against the light."

The story is as enigmatic as its two protagonists. Vincent meets the girl when she enters the gallery in the despondent hope of selling her painting which was apparently done in the secure confines of a mental hospital. Too preoccupied to pay her much attention, Waters asks the girl to leave her address, and agrees to send her a check amounting to thirty dollars for the painting. The address, however, turns out to be only "D. J.—Y. M. C. A." which is far too cryptic a guide to tracking down a young woman in New York. He takes the painting back to his basement apartment and eventually begins to form a certain identification between himself and the picture's provocative content, consisting of "a headless figure in a monklike robe reclining complacently on top a tacky vaudeville trunk; in one hand she held a flaming blue candle, in another a miniature gold cage, and her severed head lay bleeding at her feet: it was the girl's head, but here her hair was long, very long, and a snowball kitten with crystal spitfire eyes playfully pawed, as it would a spool of yarn, the sprawling ends. The wings of a hawk, headless, scarlet-breasted, copper clawed, curtained the background like a nightfall sky."

There can be little question but that the headless girl reclining on the vaudeville trunk represents the mentally ill D. J., whose aimless peregrinations have extended from New Orleans to New York. Nor can there be much doubt that the headless hawk is a representation of Vincent Waters himself, for the reader is told that Waters also is not emotionally fit; he has, like D. J., absorbed a succession of painfully thwarted quests. He finds himself at the age of thirty-six "a man of the sea, fifty miles from shore; a victim, born to be murdered, either by himself or another; an actor unemployed." He is furthermore, and by his own admission, "a poet who had never written poetry, a painter who had never painted, a lover who had never loved . . . someone, in short, without direction, and quite headless." As one of those who, again in the words from *Job*, "Know not the light," Vincent is depicted early in the story "tap-tap-tapping" with his umbrella-cane down the sidewalk in the manner of a blind man. Later, in an act of self-destruction, Vincent impulsively stabs the hawk's heart with a pair of scissors, causing the canvas to flake dried paint on the floor.

Like "The Walls Are Cold," "A Mink of One's Own," and "Miriam," "The Headless Hawk" centers upon mental and emotional disintegration, although D. J. proceeds further and more permanently over the line of irrationality than Capote's

earlier characters had. "The Headless Hawk" also illustrates
Capote's growing interest in characters with no particular
concrete identity, for, like the child Miriam, D. J. seemingly has
no origins, and is on the loose in New York. She does as Miriam
does, moves in on a person she does not know and who does not
know her. Waters never discovers D. J.'s true name or her
background, but regards her with the same "feeling he's had as a
child toward carnival freaks."

D.J.'s shadowy references to a certain Mr. Destronelli suggest
that this person, somehow connected with her mental hospital
experiences, is another of Capote's wizard men whose foreboding
presence is felt in the story even though he never appears. If
"The Headless Hawk" were not so consistently dark and
pathetic, it would, in its outward characteristics, be not so far
removed from the setting and tone of *Breakfast at Tiffany's*
where the character of Holly Golightly can be recognized as a
cheerful, delightfully self-possessed D. J.

Instead, the story has certain technical and structural flaws
that prevent its being the finished piece of fiction that it might
have been. It is, for one thing, full of details that appear to have
no function in the story as a whole. The reader may wonder, for
example, why he finds Vincent Waters absorbed in a story by
James Thurber in an old issue of *The New Yorker,* and why he
observes the same character taking such an unusually narcissistic
pleasure in his own nakedness. Why does Waters pay twenty-five
cents to view the moon and stars? What is the function of Ruby
the popcorn man? Such apparently nonessential tag ends detract
from the story's real center: Vincent's lonely and vacant urban
existence, his "talents unexploited, voyages never taken, promises unfulfilled," as well as his many abortive love affairs with
men and women alike. Neither is there the slightest ray of
illumination leading to self-understanding in the hopelessly
confused mind of D. J., who, like her friend Waters, becomes
more pitiable (if not tending to invite sympathy) as the story
reaches its conclusion.

Capote once revealed that "Shut a Final Door" was one of his
favorites among the short stories,[3] and the reasons for his
preference are not difficult to ascertain. Unlike "The Headless
Hawk," it has both thematic and tonal control, as well as a keener
sense of purpose and direction. Nevertheless, there is an element
in "Shut a Final Door" that evades rational explanation, for the

story centers around a character named Walter Ranney, an unsuccessful businessman who receives two unnerving and sinister long-distance telephone calls. His anonymous caller possesses an uncanny ability to reach him in unlikely and far removed places. The caller reaches him once in New York ("Oh, you know me, Walter. You've known me a long time"), and locates him again in the hotel room belonging to a club-footed woman under scrutiny at a medical convention in Saratoga. This aura of mystery, as unexplained as the child in "Miriam" or the character of D. J. in "The Headless Hawk," is by no means untypical of the perplexing enigmas present in most of Capote's writing.

The most imposing theme of the story is failure, and, although such earlier characters as Mrs. Miller and Vincent Waters were also in one sense or another portraits in failure, Walter Ranney's propensity for losing life's battles is drawn into sharper focus than had been the case with these and other earlier characters. At the beginning of "Shut a Final Door" Ranney has managed to alienate his friend Anna by gossiping about her. After that, he spoils his relationship with another woman (Margaret) when he becomes an assistant in an advertising house and fawns too much on the boss (who subsequently fires him). The reader learns that as a child Ranney had been caught plagiarizing a poem that he had published in the school magazine under his own name. On another occasion he had blatantly provoked a homosexual liaison, only to jump into a waiting taxi, slam the door, lean out a window, and laugh contemptuously at the man he had allowed to follow him for several blocks: "the look on his face, it was awful, it was like Christ." About his friend Rosa Cooper, he had apparently leaked the erroneous information to Walter Winchell's newspaper column that "big shot ad exec Walter Ranney and dairy heiress Rosa Cooper are telling intimates to start buying rice." To all appearances, he thrives on failure: "It was like the time he'd failed algebra and felt so relieved, so free: failure was definite, a certainty, and there is always peace in certainties."

Beyond the emphasis on failure is the almost unendurable isolation that Walter Ranney, as well as a number of his fictional predecessors, has been forced to withstand. At the outset of the story he is at his nadir, installed in a hot and seamy little New Orleans hotel room, eating peanut butter crackers, washing them down with a finger of Four Roses, and finally vomiting in a wastebasket. Like Saul Bellow's Tommy Wilhelm in *Seize the Day,* Ranney is the pitiably isolated and unloved loser who is forced eventually to own up to the reality of his condition, for he sees that "no matter what you did or how hard you tried, it all came finally to zero."

A substantial number of Capote's stories have what, for want of a better term, can be called grotesques. It was Vincent Waters in "The Headless Hawk" who found that he could love only those who had "a little something wrong [or] broken" about them, and "Shut a Final Door" has its share of such people. Margaret, for example, with her bulging eyes and her teeth reddened by lipstick, dresses like a ten-year-old child. Her friend Irving looks "like a little boy playing grownup," his legs too short to reach the footrest on a barstool. Others are still more within the category of the comic-grotesque. Rosa's companion Anna Stimson is "almost six feet tall, wore black suits, affected a monocle, a walking cane, and pounds of jingling Mexican silver." Stimson's son by a former husband ("Buck Strong, the horse-opera idol") is currently incarcerated in a "corrective academy" for having stolen from Woolworths, throwing things, and taking "potshots out the window with a .22." At a bar in Saratoga, Ranney encounters such "summer-season grotesques" as "sagging silver-foxed ladies, and little stunted jockeys." Chief among the grotesques, however, is the unnamed woman afflicted with a club foot who explains that "my doctor's . . . going to talk about me and my foot on account of I'm pretty special." Because all of the other hotel rooms are occupied, Ranney accepts an invitation to share hers. It is here that the anonymous telephone call reaches him, after which he clutches her in dismay. Her comment is to the point: "we're awfully alone in this world, aren't we?" Thus in each of Capote's stories discussed to this point (1947), the chance encounters that happen lead to emotionally debilitating results. For when last seen, Walter Ranney is, like Louise in "The Walls Are Cold," pushing his face into a pillow in a final gesture of anguish. Indications are that, just as the demonic child in "Miriam" is a projection of Mrs. Miller herself, the sinister long-distance telephone caller is in reality an expression of Ranney's conscience and his fear.

"Master Misery" is another of the New York group of stories dealing in failure and broken dreams. Its protagonist, a young woman named Sylvia, lives for a time with her friends Henry and Estelle (a Columbia law student and his wife), whose "trouble" in Sylvia's estimation, "was that they were excruciatingly married." But Sylvia has other problems. She loses her dreary job as a typist for an underwear manufacturing company known as Snug Fare, sells her watch, her beaver coat, her gold mesh evening bag, and finally, her dreams. Having moved into a depressingly furnished room in the East Sixties, she has fallen into the company of an ex-clown, the hopeless alcoholic Mr. Oreilly, whose spiritual bankruptcy parallels her own. Walking the crowded streets of Manhattan, she sees on different occasions the symbol of herself and Oreilly; in the window of a Madison Avenue shop she encounters "a life-sized, mechanical Santa Claus" who slaps his stomach and rocks "back and forth in a frenzy of electrical mirth." In the same window at a later time Sylvia and Oreilly find another exhibit that is no less suggestive; this time it is "a plastic girl with intense glass eyes [sitting] astride a bicycle pedaling at the maddest pace" and although "its wheel spokes [spin] hyp-notically, the bicycle never [moves]."

In need both of money and spiritual "meaning" in her life, Sylvia overhears a conversation between two men at an Automat, to the effect that a certain Mr. A. F. Revercomb on East Seventy-eight Street is a broker in dreams ("regular night-time dreams"), and will pay, according to their intrinsic merit, cash for the disclosure of anybody's dream experiences. Revercomb, whose name denotes his occupation, has no dreams of his own, as suggested by his very appearance: His "flat gray eyes planted like seed in the anonymity of his face and sealed within steel-dull lenses." Revercomb, however, is no fraud; he knows the real dream-article from mere imaginary fabrications of dreams.

Oreilly, however, recognizes Revercomb for what he really is, another version of the wizard man (although not referred to as such); the dream broker is "the same fellow," says Oreilly, that Sylvia must have been aware of as a child. "All mothers tell their kids about him," Oreilly says. "He lives in hollows of trees, he comes down chimneys late at night, he lurks in graveyards, and you can hear his step in the attic. The sonofabitch, he is a thief and a threat: he will take everything you have and end by leaving you nothing, not even a dream." Sylvia *is* aware of Revercomb's identity: "My family called him something else. But I can't remember what." Oreilly knows him as Master Misery.

Sylvia and Oreilly share the same world of loneliness, stress, and unproductivity that is captured in the fragments of the newspaper headline before her: *"Lana Denies, Russia Rejects, Miners Conciliate."* The external New York scene, with its frigid temperatures, snow and ice, contribute to the sense of desolation that they both feel. Sylvia's childhood friend, Estelle, feels that her predicament would be solved if she were to get married. ("I'm here to tell you, honey, that there is nothing like lying in bed at night with a man's arms around you and. . . .") But the man that Sylvia was to marry, whoever that might be, "must've fallen down a manhole," for every ostensible candidate for marriage that she has identified in New York "who seemed the slightest bit attractive was either married, too poor to get married, or queer." Her desperation causes her to lose track of reality for short periods, and her signs of emotional instability are not dissimilar to Capote's other women characters introduced earlier.

Oreilly, too, is reminiscent of certain other emotionally depleted characters in Capote's earlier fiction, not the least of whom are Vincent Waters and Walter Ranney. He has sought a number of solutions to his spiritual dilemma, as hinted at in the song he jauntily sings: *"cherryberry, moneyberry, happyberry pie, but the best old pie is a loveberry pie. . . ."* Later in the story he changes the ending of his song to "the best old pie is a whiskeyberry pie!" Irretrievably alcoholic, Oreilly has sold all his dreams to Master Misery and used the money to satisfy his habit and also, he hopes, to create a few more marketable dreams. When "you get a couple of bucks," he tells Sylvia, "you rush to the nearest liquor store—or the nearest sleepingpill machine." When he runs out of cash, he either borrows more money or steals the whiskey he is seeking. Realizing that alcoholism is Oreilly's last hold on life, Sylvia is last seen slipping a five dollar bill into his pocket as she kisses him. And when, in the story's final paragraph, two boys emerge from a bar and stare menacingly in her direction, she knows she is no longer afraid because "there was nothing left to steal."

Still, there is nothing particularly pathological about Sylvia's morbid depression and loneliness. Her former job at the underwear company (where in a single day she has typed some ninety-seven letters) is no more pointless than the plastic girl in the storefront who monotonously spins the wheels of her bicycle, but goes nowhere. Equally devoid of meaning, to her mind, is the delusion of marital harmony and bliss as represented by her struggling married friends. Only in her dreams, the essentials of which are kept hidden in a music box, can she arrive at any possibility of meaning. Eventually, however, her dreams are extracted from her by Revercomb for money, and she is left with nothing. The difficulty of Sylvia's facing another day is emphasized by the "disorganized version of 'Oh How I Hate To Get Up in the Morning'" that emanates from within her music box.

There is nothing amusing in "Master Misery," but the same cannot be said with respect to "Among the Paths to Eden" which is a dark tale with oddly humorous overtones. It is also one of the simpler, more anecdotal of the Capote stories. The scene is a huge cemetery in Queens which, besides being a haven for the deceased, offers "an unhindered view of Manhattan's skyline" for the living. On a chilly and windy day in March, a fifty-one-year-old Jew named Ivor Belli arrives at the cemetery bearing "a fine mass of jonquils" to place at the grave of his wife who had once been "a woman of many natures, most of them trying." His motive for coming out this day is less to pay tribute to his wife's memory than it is an opportunity to breathe the fresh air. He wishes also to be able to assure his two married daughters that he has paid his respects to their mother.

As he stoops "to jam the jonquils into a rock urn," he takes a certain secret comfort in the knowledge that "the woman's tongue was finally stilled." Turning to leave the gravesite, Belli encounters a husband-stalker who introduces herself as Mary O'Meaghan who detains him by feeding him peanuts while she leads him to believe that she has come to the cemetery to visit the grave of her father. Her late father, however, has "absolutely refused" burial, and has been cremated and left "at home." After some preliminary ploys, Mary O'Meaghan emphasizes her prowess as a cook and then launches into an imitation of Helen Morgan while perched on the late Sarah Belli's gravestone. This much accomplished, she comes to her point by asking Belli "a very personal question," to wit, if he had "considered marrying again." With twenty-seven years of matrimony behind him, Belli replies in all candor that that much marriage is "enough for any lifetime." But by this time, her inattention to his words is revealed by "her eyes [that] played hookey, [roaming] as though she were hunting at a party for a different, more promising face." Finally, "a new pilgrim, just entering through the gates of the cemetery" attracts her interest, while Belli takes the opportunity to make as graceful an exit as the occasion allows. He thanks Mary O'Meaghan for the peanuts and wishes her good luck.

Mary, as eccentric and as uninhibited as she is, evinces the desperate, underlying loneliness of certain other of Capote's earlier women characters. Capote, however, does not allow the pathos of Mary O'Meaghan to preclude a slight comic effect, for while Mary is not altogether unattractive, she wears "shoes which were of the sturdy, so-called sensible type," and "her chunky cheeks" assert themselves "under a drab felt hat." Although Belli does not view her as obese, neither can he "imagine that she mounted scales too cheerfully."

Consistent with a number of Capote's short stories, "Among the Paths to Eden" develops from the moment when complete strangers meet and interact. The idea of matrimonial disharmony, a not unusual element in his fiction, is present here, as well. The apparent significance of the title is in itself matrimonial in implication inasmuch as the story concerns itself primarily with Mary's effort to locate a husband who, for as much time as remains, will suffice as her Adam. For the time being, however, she has taken the wrong path toward her dreams of Edenic bliss.

Nor is there anything blissful about the digressive "Mojave," which did not appear until the June, 1975 issue of *Esquire*. "Mojave" is a different kind of a story which examines with still greater intensity (and far less whimsy) the ironic complications of mature love relationships. The story has a point to make, and that point is reinforced a number of times. It is articulated, however, only toward the conclusion: "We all, sometimes, leave each other out there under the skies. And we never understand why." "Mojave" does not suggest "why," but it does explore the theme of love and its betrayal to a considerable extent.

The protagonist is Sarah Whitelaw, thirty-six, wife of the wealthy New Yorker George Whitelaw, fifteen years older than she, and a man who "had graduated third in his class at Yale Law School, never practiced law but had gone on to top his class at Harvard Business School, [and who] had been offered a Presidential Cabinet post, and an ambassadorship to England or France, or wherever he wanted." Married at the age of twenty-

four, two months after the death of her father, Sarah had once
seen in George the approximation of "her great lost love"—her
father. Nevertheless, the opening scene of "Mojave" finds Sarah
Whitelaw in the midst of one of her regular acts of infidelity with
the oafish Dr. Ezra Bentsen, "formerly her psychoanalyst and
presently her lover." But after George Whitelaw, Ezra Bentsen is
an unlikely sexual partner ("two hundred and twenty pounds of
shortish, fiftyish, frizzly-haired, hip-heavy, myopic Manhattan
Intellectual") whom Sarah actively loathes.

It is her husband she loves, and betrays, for the company of
Bentsen, whose greed demands that she present him with
expensive gifts at each of their trysts, until she breaks their
liaison. Meanwhile, Bentsen has told Sarah of the breach that
erupted the previous evening between himself and his child-
psychiatrist wife: "I slapped Thelma. But good. And I punched
her in the stomach, too." Sarah's mind had earlier ranged over a
not-unrelated incident that had happened to her the day before:
Jaime Sanchez, her hairdresser, has told her that he intends to
murder his homosexual companion Carlos, a dentist, because
Carlos has fallen in love with Sanchez's cousin Angelita. But
Carlos does not fully comprehend Sanchez's admonition to him:
"You love or you do not. You destroy or you do not."

When George Whitelaw enters the story, he tells Sarah about
the summer after he left Yale when he had hitch-hiked to New
Mexico and California. He goes on to say that he had met an
abandoned, seventy-year-old blind man named George Schmidt
on the highway in the Mojave desert. Schmidt had told him a
story of his betrayal by two women, one of whom (the ex-
stripper Ivory Hunter, his wife) was responsible for his
abandonment "helpless, in the middle of nowhere." But whereas
Schmidt is wary of women ("women are like flies: they settle on
sugar or shit"), he is also understanding ("a woman can do you
like that, and still you love her").

George Whitelaw, it develops, has betrayed his wife Sarah, but
not without her aid, "for when they had stopped sleeping
together, they had been discussing together—indeed, col-
laborating on—each of his affairs." Neither is his involvement
with other women without its consequences, for it has triggered
still other betrayals:

Alice Kent: five months; ended because she demanded he divorce and marry her. Sister Jones: terminated after one year when her husband found out about it. Pat Simpson: a *Vogue* model who had gone to Hollywood, promised to return and never had. Adele O'Hara: beautiful, and alcoholic, a rambunctious scene-maker; he had broken that one off himself. Mary Campbell. Mary Chester. Jane Vere-Jones. Others. And now, Christine.

If the truth be known, however, George Whitelaw feels secretly "emasculated by women."

The relation between "Mojave" and some of Capote's earlier work is apparent enough. Although "Mojave" is basically a story of New York, it contains scenes of the Southwest that echo some of his earlier excursions into local color fiction. In that part of the country, he writes, "there wasn't any shade. Nothing but sand and mesquite and this boiling blue sky." The character Freddy Feo, who takes up with Ivory Hunter, is a carry-over from another Capote character, Tico Feo, the prisoner in "A Diamond Guitar" (1950). Both Tico and Freddy are closely identified with guitars decorated in rhinestone. Capote's attention to problems related to homosexuality (such as exists in *Other Voices, Other Rooms* and *In Cold Blood*) is evidenced once again in the strained relations between Jaime and Carlos, as well as in Freddy Feo, recently hired by a trailer park manager who "had picked him up in one of those fag bars in Cat City and put him to work as a handyman."

Capote's fascination with snow, a symbol of isolation and estrangement in such works as *Other Voices, Other Rooms* and in the short story "Master Misery," is again present in "Mojave." When, for example, Sarah and George embrace, "the flesh against her lips felt as cold as the snowflakes at the window." In the next-to-last paragraph in the story the heavy silk window draperies in the Whitelaws' apartment conceal "the night river and the lighted riverboats, so snow-misted that they were as muted as the design in a Japanese scroll of winter night."

The New York stories are those in which a cold, impersonal, and uncongenial environment seems to foster characters who are, in the main, the victims of loneliness, alienation, and despair. As a consequence, their behavior not infrequently hovers somewhere between the engagingly eccentric and the certifiably deranged. Generally humorless, the New York fiction lacks some of the occasional warmth and familiarity that is often (but certainly not always) present in Capote's southern stories.

II *Stories of the South*

The earliest (1944) of these is "The Shape of Things" which, like "A Mink of One's Own," is a wartime narrative. It brings four characters together on a moving train somewhere between the Carolinas and Virginia. Three of them are related directly in one sense or another to the war itself, and they are brought in touch with one another on a railway diner for a brief interlude that is perhaps more felt than articulated. The three consist of "a ruddy-cheeked marine and a heart-faced girl" (his wife), as well as a severely battle-fatigued corporal from the Army. The fourth character, and the central one, is "a wispish-sized, white pompadoured woman" who, at least ostensibly, has no relation to the war and its attendant human dilemmas. She regards the girl (who comes from Alabama) merely as a "war bride." When the corporal suddenly makes his appearance in the dining car and lurches "awkwardly toward them and [collapses] in the table's empty seat like a rag," she regards him as a drunk. The marine, by contrast to the woman, understands the corporal's condition and evinces some degree of sympathetic understanding: "Listen, fella, you better get a doctor." The corporal, in spite of his erratic, nervous behavior, is aware of his own condition and attempts to reveal this understanding to the other three by saying "D'ya think I want to sit down at a table with . . . someone like you and make 'em sick? D'ya think I want to scare a kid like this one over here and put ideas in her head about her own guy! I've been waiting months, and they tell me I'm well, but the first time . . ." With this somewhat stilted outburst he bolts out of the diner, leaving the three alone again. The white-pompadoured woman's response to this is merely to pay for the coffee that the corporal has left behind.

Capote also used the unifying device of characters brought together on a train in his next story, "A Tree of Night," although the implications of "The Shape of Things" are quite different. In the latter story the central idea is one that is anything but unusual in war-related literature—William Faulkner had used it in *Soldiers' Pay* in 1926, for example—that persons like the white-pompadoured woman who are well insulated from the unspeakable realities of war seem unable or unwilling to comprehend the effects of war upon those who have been touched directly by it. "The Shape of Things" is therefore partly an exercise in point of view wherein the woman is somewhat ironically unable to imagine the grave predicaments faced by others in her midst, and reacts mostly by silence and indignation.

As a short story, "A Tree of Night" succeeds much more than "The Shape of Things" for a number of reasons. It is, first of all, well sustained in its tone. The icicles that are suspended from the remote southern railway depot at night, are "like some crystal monster's vicious teeth," and they establish the prevailing mood for the rest of the narration. On the lonely railway platform it is windy, cold, and dark, except for "a string of naked light bulbs." As the story's protagonist, a college sophomore named Kay, climbs aboard the last remaining dingy railway coach, the gloom of the deserted depot extends to the tawdriness of the coach's interior, with its disarray of partly eaten sandwiches, remnants of apples and oranges, discarded paper cups, newspapers, and soft drink bottles—all of which combine with the staleness of tobacco smoke, the prospect of dozing travellers, and a leaking water-cooler to produce a singularly depressing scene.

The story traces the gradual undoing of Kay, who is finally coerced into surrendering the contents of her purse to a hypnotically grotesque pair of travelling con-artists. The man and woman who with ironic subtlety break her will as she falls into a macabre trance, accomplish their ends not only by their relentless insistence, but also by the lighting on the train and by the cadence of the moving locomotive. Kay, a nineteen-year-old, is on her way back to college after having attended the funeral of an uncle who has willed her a green Western guitar. Her decidedly funereal point of view is heightened by other elements in the story, such as the ghoulish monster teeth suspended from the station house and the gloom of entering the coffin-like interior of the last coach on this dreary, nocturnal passenger train. Kay settles in the car's only vacant seat where across from her are situated the two con-artists, she in her lavender hat with its cluster of celluloid cherries drooping from it, he deaf and dumb. Their game, as it turns out, is the reenactment of live burial for the entertainment of the curious in "every tank town in the South." The woman's advertising handbill comes, no doubt, as an unpleasant reminder of the funeral from which Kay has just returned:

LAZARUS
The Man Who Is Buried Alive
A Miracle
See For Yourself
Adults, 25¢ ———— Children, 10¢

With a description that invites comparison with Eudora Welty's
story "Petrified Man," the eccentric woman explains to Kay their
routine reenactment of his mock funeral: "*He* wears a gorgeous
made-to-order bridegroom suit and a turban and lotsa talcum on
his face," she states matter-of-factly. "After the hymn, after the
sermon, we bury him." The deaf-mute, she says, has the ability to
lie motionless for hours in a coffin by putting himself into a
hypnotic trance. Then people come to view him in a storefront
window. "Stays there all night stiff as a poker and people come
and look: scares the livin' hell out of 'em. . . ." The details of
their act are ludicrous, even funny, except that both the present
moment and certain of Kay's sinister childhood memories each
conspire against her, breaking her will. The coldness of the car's
platform makes her head ache, and outside the coach window
the tall trees seem "misty, painted pale by a malicious
moonshine." The stars overhead remind the reader of the stars
painted on the lid of the mute's casket, and the mute himself
recalls for Kay the white image of her dead uncle's head resting
on its casket pillow.
    She is reminded too, and this is central to the story's
"meaning," of her childhood memories "of terrors that once,
long ago, had hovered above her like haunted limbs on a tree of
night," and of "the unfailing threat of the wizard man." For her,
the mute quite obviously becomes the living embodiment of the
dreaded wizard man of her girlhood imagination. His desire is to
sell her a love charm in the form of a shellacked peach seed. Too
terrified either to ask the railway conductor to find her another
seat, or to cry out and thus awaken the deathlike slumber of
those around her, she submits, pulling her raincoat up "like a
shroud" as the woman takes possession of Kay's purse.
    "A Tree of Night" contains certain ironic elements, not the
least of which is the complete surrender of an apparently
rational and intelligent young college woman to the purely
emotional forces of the moment and to the wiles of an
exceedingly crude (and yet not unskilled), partially drunken,

self-proclaimed fraud and her afflicted partner who utters not a single word. In spite of Kay's protestations, she is emotionally seduced into cooperating with the couple when the woman tries to force her to drink some cheap gin, although Kay finally manages to pour the paper cup of gin into the sound hole of her green guitar.

Other ironic details are also present; at one point the woman admonishes Kay for not telling the truth when Kay has tried to break away, allegedly to meet a friend on the same train; it is the woman and her accomplice, of course, who trade professionally in lies. The woman then suggests that for Kay to leave her seat would hurt the mute's feelings. Only a page later, however, the woman notes that her companion is immune to having his feelings trampled on by incredulous "smart alecks" because "he's afflicted." A short time later the woman hoists her skirt and blows her nose enthusiastically on the ragged hem of her petticoat, only to rearrange her skirt "with considerable primness." As for the rest of the passengers seated in this veritable mobile garbage dump rolling through a siege of foul weather in a dimly lit and offensive-smelling antiquated railway car, they seem "not . . . at all conscious of any discomfort" because they are asleep.

The story is made coherent by a series of leitmotifs and images. The most imposing of these is the awareness of death as suggested by entombment, morbid fear of supernatural forces, bodies, shrouds, and caskets. Another recurring image in the tale is that of devoured fruit. On the floor of the coach are apple cores and orange hulls. The lacquered peach seed that the mute desires to palm off on Kay is another such image, as is the cluster of faintly comic artificial cherries that are sewn to the woman's hat. Such images are but a reminder of the otherwise spent and artificial atmosphere that engulfs the whole narrative, particularly the funeral that Kay has just witnessed, and later the gloomy interior of the coach. The result of these unpleasant experiences for her is but another step in the loss of her youthful innocence.

Capote's early fiction is characterized in part by an unevenness in artistic quality. There is probably no better illustration of this than the differences that exist between "A Tree of Night" and "Preacher's Legend," both of which appeared in 1945. The deficiencies of "Preacher's Legend" lie in both its narrative style

and its dubious thematic import. The story centers around "an
old colored man" of advanced age ("ninety or a hundred,
maybe") who lives alone in the rural South and who is
preoccupied by the passing of his wife Evelina long ago, as well
as by certain fundamentalist religious persuasions. At one
juncture in the story he retires alone into the woods to pray at a
location known to him simply as The Place. But when he opens
his Bible, clasps his hands, and lifts his head, he is interrupted by
two sinister white hunters bearing a slain wildcat. The hunters
are identified only as Curly Head and Yellow Hair. Owing to his
generally confused state and to his preoccupation with the Bible
(despite the Preacher's illiteracy), "he knew who the strangers
were—knew it from the Good Book." Accordingly, he addresses
one of the hunters as "Mistuh Jesus," and the other as "Mistuh
Saint," evidently believing that the two have come to deliver
him to his heavenly reward.

But Preacher is not ready to go. To Mistuh Jesus he says, "I'se
been turnin' de whole mattah ovah an' I'se come to conclude I
don't wants to go wid y'all." Curly Head and Yellow Hair do not
take the old black man seriously, and are of the opinion that "he's
just been sitting in the sun too long, that's all." As the two make
their departure, however, Preacher asks Mistuh Jesus to do him
one favor: "If you can see yo' way clear to do me one mo' favuh,
I'd 'preciate it if you evah gits de time iffen you'd find my ol'
woman . . . names Evelina . . . an' say hello from Preacher an'
tells her what a good happy man I is." Curly Head promises to
fulfill Preacher's request "first thing in the morning," but as the
two hunters make their way down the road they burst into
derisive laughter.

The story has relatively little to say. Capote reveals something
of Preacher's private world, a world of myth and memory that is
contrasted in the story with some harsher realities of the
intrusive "outside" world of violence and cynicism represented
by the two hunters. Preacher's remarks to himself, and to them,
make the narrative partly a dialect story, and the Preacher
himself is sketched in the tradition of the childlike, subservient,
equivocal black man of the Uncle Remus stories.

Some of Capote's early interest in the gothic mode that found
its flowering in *Other Voices, Other Rooms* is to be found in
"Preacher's Legend," just as in "A Tree of Night." Evelina had
been "dead and buried two springs ago," and Preacher is mindful

that some of his own children have gone "to their graves" and that "on the eve of his puppy's death, it was said, a great red-winged bird with a fearsome beak had sailed into the room from nowhere." Other images and suggestions reinforce the morose tone of the narration. From his wall stares "a wonderful poster-picture of a golden-haired girl holding a bottle of NE-HI [that is] torn at the mouth, so that her smile was wicked and leering." Outside, meanwhile, a rooster crows and the dogwood blossoms. Preacher recalls Evelina's admonition to him against believing in spirits: ("I ain't gonna listen to no mo' of dat spook talk."). And yet, when he first hears the approach of the hunters in the woods, he regards them as apparitions. Such details as these point to the story's affinity with local color tradition as evidenced by its whole cultural milieu, its rural southern setting, its reuse of black colloquialisms, and its somewhat paternalistic view of the black man.

After "Preacher's Legend," comedy prevailed in Capote's southern stories, and one of the better comic tales is "My Side of the Matter" which is written (uncharacteristically for Capote) in the first person. The narrator is a seriocomic sixteen-year-old bridegroom and expectant father who, to his infinite regret, has been persuaded to relinquish his "swell position clerking at the Cash'n'Carry to accompany his bride to her aunts' house in Admiral's Mill" which, he says, "is nothing but a damn gap in the road any way you care to consider it."

Domestic differences of opinion have culminated in his being attacked by his wife Marge's two aunts. One of them, Eunice, has threatened him with a Civil War sword, and the other (Olivia-Ann) has brandished a "fourteen-inch hog knife" against him. The result of these disputes is the young man's barricading himself in the family parlor by pushing heavy furniture against the doors, locking the windows, and lowering the shades. Last seen, he is "munching a juicy, creamy, chocolate cherry" from out of a "five pound box of Sweet Love candy." As his would-be attackers plead for him to surrender, his reply is to give them "a tune on the piano every now and then just to let them know" that he is still "cheerful."

The story is as light and comic as most of the others were dark and serious, and yet throughout his career Capote persists in concentrating upon the grotesque characters he had used before, except that in "My Side of the Matter" they are devoted to comic ends. Here the narrator himself admits to being "slightly stocky," but he attributes that to his not having "got [his] full growth yet." Eunice, seeing him in a less understanding light, regards him merely as "the runt of the litter." But Marge protests: "you seem to forget, Aunt Olivia-Ann, that this is my husband, the father of my unborn child." Eunice then makes a nasty sound. "Well, all I can say is I most certainly wouldn't be bragging about it."

The other characters are scarcely more appealing. Marge, the child bride, according to her husband, "has no looks, no body, and no brains whatever," and on top of those shortcomings, "ups and gets pregnant" after the couple are betrothed less than three months. Eunice, on the other hand, has "a behind that must weight [sic] a tenth of a ton," and tries vainly to chew her tobacco with ladylike decorum. Olivia-Ann, according to the sixteen-year-old, is worse still, "for she is a natural-born half-wit and ought really to be kept in somebody's attic." To make matters worse, he says, "she's real pale and skinny and has a mustache. She squats around most of the time whittling on a stick with her fourteen-inch hog knife."

The women make no pretense about their disapproval of the young man, compelling him as they do to sleep apart from his wife on a cot erected on the screenless back porch, which is besieged both by mosquitoes "that could murdeı a buffalo" and by "dangerous flying roaches and a posse of local rats big enough to haul a wagon train." With continued vehemence, the women accuse him of ineptitude and outright laziness. Says Eunice, "if you think I'd let that runt drive my just-as-good-as-brand-new 1934 Chevolet as far as the privy and back you must've gone clear out of your head." Alluding to his laziness, she continues, "if he's ever so much as driven a plow I'll eat a dozen gophers fried in turpentine."

The humor of the tale is at once sophisticated and slapstick, for while the narrator retains an astutely ironic point of view throughout, he also speaks with an ingenious crudity. In the end, the story turns into a free-for-all. Marge hands Eunice a Civil War sword with which to restrain the narrator, while Olivia-Ann rushes into the yard bellowing "The Battle Hymn of the Republic." The effect of all this is hilarious Faulknerian fun, as pointless, perhaps, as it is funny.

Like a number of stories before and after it, "My Side of the

Matter" concerns a less-than-welcome guest in an alien house-hold, a circumstance that Capote uses in such stories as "Miriam," "The Headless Hawk," "Shut a Final Door," "Master Misery," as well as in *Other Voices, Other Rooms*. And although the young man's involuntary exile in "My Side of the Matter" is comic, he is still another of Capote's isolated and unloved outcasts.

"Jug of Silver" is another comic story, and the chief difference between it and "My Side of the Matter" is that the former is a much more charming narrative, though no less enigmatic in its message. It is the story of a waifish boy known only as Appleseed who is credited with guessing the amount of money ($77.35, in all) contained in a gallon jug that had once contained "store-bought" Italian wine.

The scene is a small town in the deep South where the narrator, looking fondly back to his boyhood, recalls Mr. Ed Marshall, his uncle, "a squat, square-faced, pinkfleshed man with looping, manly white mustaches" who owns and manages the Valhalla drugstore. Early in the story Marshall appears as "a renowned teetotaler" drinking red wine with his companion, a somewhat mysterious, supposedly Egyptian, dentist named Hamurabi who unaccountably possesses no foreign accent, and who, in the opinion of the narrator, "wasn't any more Egyptian than the man in the moon." Marshall, a little tipsy from the wine, and a great deal concerned about the sudden appearance of an old man named Rufus McPherson who has opened a rival drugstore across the town square, decides to fill the jug with nickels and dimes. His idea is to promote business by allowing his customers to estimate the value of the jug's contents, and to award the same contents on Christmas eve to the nearest estimator. To Hamurabi, the jug represents "the pot at the end of the rainbow," but to Marshall, it is a sensational piece of business promotion. He tells his customers that "the more you buy, the more chances you get. And I'll keep all guesses in a ledger till Christmas Eve, at which time whoever comes closest to the right amount will get the whole shebang."

The plan succeeds enormously. "Why," the narrator says, "the Valhalla hadn't done so much business since Station Master Tully, poor soul, went stark raving mad and claimed to have discovered oil back of the depot, causing the town to be overrun with wildcat prospectors." But moral and sentimental problems confront Marshall and Hamurabi when Appleseed arrives on the scene and claims to live on a farm outside the town limits. Appleseed also claims to be twelve years old, but his sister Middy ("a said looking kid" who resembles "a regular bean pole" and who has something wrong with her teeth) says that her brother is only eight. Obviously down on his luck, Appleseed never changes his outfit which consists of "a red sweater, blue denim britches, and a pair of man-sized boots that went clop clop with every step." His mother, he says, weighs but seventy-four pounds, his brother plays the fiddle at weddings for a fee of fifty cents, and his father is apparently one short step ahead of the sheriff.

Appleseed resolves to ascertain the correct amount contained in the jug, but instead of taking a mere educated guess, he intends somehow to count the money: "Now, the way I got it figured, there ain't but one sure-fire thing and that's to count every nickel and dime." Hamurabi is incredulous: "Count! You better have X-ray eyes, son, that's all I can say." Moved by the sight of the pathetic boy and his even more pathetic sister, Hamurabi has not the heart to see the child's face on Christmas Eve when he, in all probability, will be grievously disappointed: "I don't want to see that kid's face. This is Christmas and I mean to have a rip-roaring time."

At the climax of the story at the Valhalla on Christmas Eve, the store fills with an anxious assemblage in only twenty minute's time. Capote's handling of the suspense element is perfectly timed. Appleseed is accorded the honor of opening an envelope containing a slip with the prize-winning figure on it, and it becomes clear that Marshall, in the spirit of yuletide charity and holiday good will, has altered the figure to coincide precisely with Appleseed's estimate. Only the town drunk who masquerades as Santa Claus and "who had a snootful by this time" causes a rumpus, although it develops that he has been paid to do so by Rufus McPherson.

The story is related with an engaging oral quality in the tradition of the American tall tale. Appleseed wins the contents of the jug, so Capote's explanation goes, because he had been fortuitously born with a caul over his head. But all this happened long ago. In the ensuing years Appleseed moved with his family to Florida and was never again heard from. In the remaining time before his death, Marshall "was invited each Christmas day to tell the story of Appleseed to the Baptist Bible class." Later, Hamurabi had recorded the "legend" of Appleseed and had attempted to interest an editor in publishing it, but was unsuccessful. Capote's story ends on still another ironic note, for the editor who had turned down Hamurabi's version of the story had done so because Hamurabi had not stressed the fact that Middy supposedly "turned out to be a movie star" after she acquired enough money to pay for false teeth. "But that's not what happened," says the narrator, "so why should you lie?" The real center of the story is, of course, predicated on Marshall's charitable distortion of the truth.

As in so many of Capote's short stories, "Jug of Silver" offers the reader an array of colorful and eccentric characters, especially in the form of precocious, determined children. The children in the story are much like those in "Children on Their Birthdays" which appeared next, and which is similar in situation, setting, and atmosphere. "Jug of Silver" also shares with a number of other stories, such as "A Tree of Night," "Miriam," and "The Headless Hawk," a certain counterrealistic quality which, if it makes the story no less believable, is still considerably removed from stark, photographic reality. It makes effective use of some genuinely warm and comic southern local color elements; but comic or not, it contains a touch of sadness growing out of the use of deprived characters that makes the texture of the narrative decidedly bittersweet.

That same bittersweetness prevails in another of Capote's favorite stories, the hilarious "Children on Their Birthdays." The tale begins and ends on a poignant note, however, for the protagonist (an enigmatic ten-year-old named Miss Lily Jane Bobbit) is eventually run over and killed by the same six o'clock bus that had originally brought her and her mother to the tiny southern town which is the scene of the narrative. The story, withal, is a remarkable piece of local color narration told by an anonymous first-person observer. Much like "My Side of the Matter," "Children on Their Birthdays" has no imposing thematic point to make, although it is rich in a variety of kinds of suggestiveness.

Structurally, the story is framed by Miss Bobbit's arrival and would-be departure, for as she runs toward "those moons of roses" prepared by her childhood friends as a going-away tribute, she runs into the path of the bus and is killed. The story itself ends on this note, and the immensely comic aspects of the story are therefore tempered.

Still, "enigmatic" is the word that applies best to Miss Bobbit's character and behavior. From the moment she makes her appearance in town, there is a certain disruption of the usual patterns of social and psychological behavior among a whole colony of provincial southern children in whom change is ultimately brought about. The "wiry little girl in a starched, lemon-colored party dress [carrying a] spinsterish umbrella" proceeds to evoke a wide range of responses (jealousy, awe, admiration, outrage, and finally love) among those children who are attentive to her. Miss Bobbit is another of Capote's somewhat disarmingly precocious child characters. The narrator's Aunt El, for one, is bothered by this ten-year-old child's wearing makeup, but aside from that, Miss Bobbit possesses an adult dignity, for "she was a lady, and, what is more, she looked you in the eye with a manlike directness."

The story consists of a series of loosely related anecdotes involving the child, each of which is progressively more comic and revealing of character. At the outset, the eccentric child moves into an eccentric-looking house, "an old dark place with about two dozen lightning rods scattered on the roof." The gossipy Mrs. Sawyer who owns the place and who is terrified by storms, spreads the rumor that the child's father, "the sweetest singing man in the whole of Tennessee," is serving time in a state penitentiary, and that Miss Bobbit and her suspiciously silent mother subsist on a raw vegetarian diet. When the child befriends a young black girl named Sister Rosalba ("baby-fat and sugar-plum shaped"), Mrs. Sawyer tells Aunt El "that it went against her grain to have a nigger lolling smack there in plain sight on her front porch." And when Miss Bobbit announces that Rosalba is to be considered as her sister, the initial racial slurs from the white population are finally discontinued. On the occasion when Miss Bobbit becomes incensed over the dogs that station themselves under her window at night and keep her awake, she and Sister Rosalba take the matter into their own hands after the sheriff refuses to do anything, and after Sister Rosalba reveals that she does not regard them as dogs at all, but as "some kind of devil." The two are "seen stalking through town carrying a flower basket filled with rocks." When they come upon a dog, Miss Bobbit scrutinizes it, and if it is one of the condemned, Sister Rosalba, "with ferocious aim, would take a rock from her basket and crack the dog between the eyes."

Later, when Miss Bobbit becomes the county subscription

representative for a list of magazines that include *"Reader's Digest, Popular Mechanics, Dime Detective* and *Child's Life,"* she enlists the help of the unruly Billy Bob and his exceedingly ornery companion who is ironically misnamed Preacher Star. Sister Rosalba, meanwhile, begins to market an assortment of cosmetics called Dewdrop, and also hires the boys to make deliveries. The work is surprisingly difficult, for "Billy Bob used to be so tired in the evening that he would hardly chew his supper." But the most comic part of the story involves the appearance of the town con-man (Manny Fox) who, in the manner of Mark Twain, promotes a show featuring a "Fan Dancer Without the Fan" as well as an array of local talent elicited from among the townspeople who will compete for "A Genuine Hollywood Screen Test." The fanless dancer (clad in a bathing suit, much to the disappointment of the local hangers-on) turns out to be none other than Mrs. Manny Fox ("A deadpan pimento-tongued redhead with wet lips and moist eyelids"), currently residing at the Chucklewood Tourist Camp.

The main attraction for the narrator and his companions is Miss Bobbit, the ladylike Miss Bobbit, who has been practicing her "act" behind drawn window shades at Mrs. Sawyer's. When another local performer (Buster Riley) has finished "Waltzing Matilda" on a saw, Miss Bobbit proceeds to shock the townfolk by singing in "a rowdy sandpaper voice": "I was born in China, and raised in Jay-pan . . . if you don't like my peaches, stay away from my can oho o-ho!" Aunt El gasps as, "with a bump [Miss Bobbit] up-ended her skirt to display her blue-lace underwear." Her act terminates in a grand flourish when "in the midst of a full split" a Roman candle bursts "into firey balls of red, white and blue," as the audience rises for her to bellow out "The Star Spangled Banner."

In the meantime, Manny Fox skips town, and after two weeks of non-action on the promised Hollywood screen test, Miss Bobbit organizes the "Manny Fox Hangman's Club" which leads eventually to his arrest in Uphill, Arkansas. For her efforts, she receives the "Good Deed Merit Award" from the Sunbeam Girls of America, of which she takes a dim view because of "all that rowdy bugle blowing." By the time the Hangman's Club proposes to send her to Hollywood for a screen test (in return for ten percent of her lifetime earnings) Billy Bob has fallen in love with Miss Bobbit. But after the farewell festivities which involve "boys in flower masked faces," she runs into the path of the bus.

Miss Bobbit, remotely the same kind of self-determined, totally independent, and enterprising child that Capote's Miriam had been, can be viewed as the forerunner of certain other characters yet to be created, not the least of which are Idabel Tomkins in *Other Voices, Other Rooms* and Holly Golightly in *Breakfast at Tiffany's.* Similarly, Billy Bob's habit of escaping up the nearest tree in moments of stress prefigures *The Grass Harp* where a whole colony of characters select the same arboreal refuge. Capote's attention to the elements of hoax and childhood problems, also evident in "Jug of Silver," foreshadows *The Thanksgiving Visitor.*

But Capote's next story in the southern group was "A Diamond Guitar" which appeared in 1950 and which belongs among the darker of his short stories. The scene is a prison farm set in the midst of a pine forest in the South, where the prisoners pass their days tapping the trees for turpentine. The protagonist is a certain Mr. Schaeffer who is serving a sentence of ninety-nine years and a day for having killed a man who, according to the omniscient narrator, "deserved to die." Schaeffer enjoys a limited measure of prestige among the prison guards and inmates, in whose eyes he has "a mask of special respect." He is literate, for one thing, and prisoners not infrequently bring letters from outside for him to read aloud, although he has the habit of improvising "more cheerful messages and does not read what is written on the page."

One Sunday a truck arrives bearing a young Cuban named Tico Feo, "a knifer" who has allegedly "cut up a sailor in Mobile" and who brings with him, among other cherished items, "a guitar studded with glass diamonds." Given to telling outlandish lies, the young Cuban causes most of the men in the green wooden sleep house to feel a kind of love for him, inspired, perhaps, by his songs sung to the accompaniment of his guitar. "Except that they did not combine their bodies or think to do so," the narrator says, "they were as lovers."

Tico reveals to Schaeffer that he has a friend named Frederico in Mobile who will put them on his boat and carry them to freedom if they can first manage to escape from the prison camp. And as Schaeffer fantasizes about his prospects for making an escape, he hears the sound of a coffin being assembled in the yard for one of the prisoners who has died. Thinks Schaeffer,

"This is for me, it is mine." But it is Tico's plan to hide in a tree until dark, and then make an escape by running through a creek and thereby leave no scent for search dogs to follow. The last act that Tico performs before attempting his escape is to put his guitar in tune. When the moment of their prison break comes, the two men run through the creek as "icy geysers [spray] around them." While Tico makes his successful escape, Schaeffer breaks an ankle when he runs into a fallen tree. The captain of the guards ironically interprets the whole episode to mean that Schaeffer has been injured in an attempt to capture Tico, for which he is honored by having his picture in the local newspaper. Tico, meanwhile, makes good on his bid for freedom, and, in his typically romantic fashion, is said to have entered the home of a spinster woman, kissed her twice, and fled.

Three winters go by, and Schaeffer's hair has become progressively whiter. He still keeps the "diamond guitar with its glass gems turning yellow with age. A new prisoner is assigned to the sleep house, and although he is said to be an accomplished guitar player, his songs come out sour, "for it was as though Tico Feo, tuning his guitar that last morning, had put a curse on it." When last seen, the guitar is beneath Schaeffer's cot, where in the night the old man "sometimes reaches it out, and his fingers drift across the strings: then, the world."

Like so many other Capote tales (such as "A Tree of Night," "Miriam," "My Side of the Matter," "The Headless Hawk," "Shut a Final Door," "Jug of Silver," and "Master Misery") "A Diamond Guitar" is set in motion when complete strangers begin to interact. Tico Feo's rather brief influence over the dreary, hopeless life of Schaeffer has provided the old man with not only a ray of hope for an eventual escape, but also some colorful memories to fuel his romantic imagination. Tico himself shares with Billy Bob (of "Children on Their Birthdays") the notion that one can find solace and safety if he will but climb a tree. But in general, Tico is another of Capote's array of fiercely independent characters who, like Miss Bobbit and Holly Golightly, are far more motivated from within than from without.

In "A Diamond Guitar," Schaeffer functions as the protagonist because he is the person to whom development occurs. And although Tico himself undergoes no significant change, the monotony of Schaeffer's life is alleviated by Tico's brief presence. Tico, with his "bottle of Evening in Paris cologne" and his "Rand McNally map of the world," enjoys a kind of life far removed from Schaeffer's; for to Tico, being alive "was to remember brown rivers where the fish run, and sunlight on a lady's hair." He leaves behind him only the diamond guitar, an emblematic reminder of himself.

The most warmly engaging of all Capote's ventures into short fiction is *A Christmas Memory* (1956), a blend of fiction and autobiography concentrating once more on the author's remembered life in the South. His powers of description in *A Christmas Memory* are quite possibly unparalleled anywhere else in his work. When the book begins, it is "a morning in late November. A coming of winter morning more than twenty years ago." Capote remembers himself at the age of seven. His guardian, "a woman with snow white hair," is at the window "wearing tennis shoes and a shapeless gray sweater over a summer calico dress," and looking like "a bantam hen." Because "it's fruitcake weather," the boy and the old woman set out in a buggy, the wheels of which "wobble like a drunkard's legs" to find the ingredients necessary to bake thirty cakes: "cherries and citron, ginger and vanilla and canned Hawaiian pineapple, rinds and raisins and walnuts and whiskey and oh, so much flour, butter, so many eggs, spices, flavorings. . . ."

Like much of his earlier fiction (such as *Other Voices, Other Rooms* and *The Grass Harp*), *A Christmas Memory* can be read as a moving expression of lost childhood innocence and idyllic simplicity. The texture of the prose is also similar to those earlier pieces, for it is both subtle and impressionistic. There is probably no better instance of this kind of writing in *A Christmas Memory* than Capote's description of a late fall southern dawn:

Morning. Frozen rime lusters the grass; the sun, round as an orange and orange as hot-weather moons, balances on the horizon, burnishes the silvered winter weeks. A wild turkey calls. A renegade hog grunts in the undergrowth. Soon, by the edge of knee-deep, rapid-running water, we have to abandon the buggy. Queenie [a dog] wades the stream first, paddles across barking complaints at the swiftness of the current, the pneumonia-making coldness of it. We follow, holding our shoes and equipment (a hatchet, a burlap sack) above our heads. A mile more: of chastising thorns, burs and briers that catch at our clothes; of rusty pine needles brilliant with gaudy fungus and melted feathers. Here, there, a flash, a flutter, an ecstasy of shrillings remind us that not all the birds have flown south. Always, the path unwinds through lemony sun pools and pitch vine tunnels. Another creek to cross: a disturbed armada of speckled trout froths the water round us, frogs the size of plates practice belly flops; beaver workmen are building a dam. On the farther shore, Queenie shakes herself and trembles. My friend [Miss Sook Faulk] shivers too: not with cold but enthusiasm. One of her hat's ragged roses sheds a petal as she lifts her head and inhales the pine-heavy hair. "We're almost there; can you smell it, Buddy?" she says, as though we were approaching an ocean.

Curiously enough, Capote once said that *A Christmas Memory* was the only piece he ever wrote "that *depended* on its southern setting. The moment I wrote that story I knew that I would never write another word about the South. I'm not going to be haunted by it anymore."[4] Haunted or not, Capote succeeded in creating in *A Christmas Memory* a high watermark of personal feeling and dramatic intensity; he recalls at one point that for Christmas he had wanted a bicycle, but that because of his guardian Miss Faulk's impoverished state, he anticipated receiving a kite (made by her), along with "socks, a Sunday school shirt, some handkerchiefs, a hand-me-down sweater and a year's subscription to a religious magazine for children." This will be the last Christmas with Miss Faulk. Her mind begins to fail, and the boy is to be sent to a series of military schools, "a miserable succession of bugle-blowing prisons, grim, reveille-ridden summer camps." Back in the present, some twenty years after these childhood experiences, he learns of her death, which he regards as a "severing [of an] irreplaceable part of [himself]." He concludes, "that is why, walking across a school campus on this particular December morning, I keep searching the sky. As if I expected to see, rather like hearts, a lost pair of kites hurrying toward heaven."

Capote's *The Thanksgiving Visitor* shares with "A Diamond Guitar" and *A Christmas Memory* not only a remote southern locality, but also a tone of wistfulness born out of the narrator's sense of profound loneliness. The narrator in *The Thanksgiving Visitor*, however, is a child, and the story itself can be read in more than one light. Perhaps the most obvious way of seeing the narrative is as a documentary of life in rural Alabama in one of the worst of the Depression years, 1932. At the climactic Thanksgiving dinner, Uncle B (one of the narrator's four guardians) offers a prayer appropriate to the occasion: "Bless

You, O Lord, for the bounty of our table, the varied fruits we can be thankful for on this Thanksgiving Day of a troubled year." Buddy, a Capote self-portrait, recalls having been fed magnificently on "cockcrow repasts of ham and fried chicken, fried pork chops, fried catfish, fried squirrel (in season), fried eggs, hominy grits with gravy, blackeyed peas, collards with collard liquor and cornbread to mush it in, biscuits, pound cake, pancakes and molasses, honey in the comb, homemade jams and jellies, sweetmilk, buttermilk, coffee chickory-flavored and hot as Hades." But he is understandably troubled by the thought of those who have to make do with less. "Throughout the Depression Years," he says, "our school distributed free milk and sandwiches to all children whose families were too poor to provide them with a lunch box." But a few children were still harder hit by the bad times: "some boys, girls too, were forced to go barefoot right through the bitterest weather—that's how hard the Depression had hit Alabama."

For Buddy, the times were also difficult, but for reasons somewhat independent of the country's depressed economy. An autobiographic story, *The Thanksgiving Visitor* is a bittersweet, retrospective, illumination of his early life with three aunts and an uncle. The protagonist is Buddy's only "friend," Miss Sook Faulk, for "as she was a child herself . . . she understood children, and understood me absolutely." Even so, Buddy's life is not an easy one, inasmuch as they "had taken me under their roof because of a disturbance among my more immediate family, a custody battle that, for involved reasons, had left me stranded in this somewhat eccentric Alabama household. Not that I was unhappy there: indeed, moments of those few years turned out to be the happiest part of an otherwise difficult childhood. . . ."

The conflict in the story centers around Buddy's unhappy relations with a twelve-year-old contemporary named Odd Henderson. "Talk about mean!" says Buddy, "Odd Henderson was the meanest human creature in my experience." Odd, who has failed the first grade twice, vents his hostilities on the more passive Buddy by knocking him to the ground and rubbing prickly cockleburs into his scalp as "a circle of kids ganged around to titter, or pretend to." Malicious acts of this nature cause Buddy to find excuses not to attend school, and when Miss Sook comprehends the problem, she develops a stratagem to solve Buddy's dilemma, while she finds a way to advance the cause of Christian charity at the same time. Convinced that Buddy must somehow "come to terms with people like Odd Henderson," Miss Sook pays a call on Molly Henderson, Odd's destitute, toothless mother who is faced with a house full of children and an absentee, jailbird husband. Miss Sook extends an invitation to Odd for Thanksgiving dinner.

The dinner itself ends in a debacle when Odd steals Miss Sook's prize cameo. At the dinner table, Buddy does what he can to expose the crime, but with continued holiday charity, Miss Sook covers up for Odd's act of petty theft. Because, in Buddy's judgment, "she'd lied to save his skin, [and] betrayed our friendship," Buddy is all the more disconsolate. Even so, the Thanksgiving invitation solved the original problem of Odd's harassment of Buddy, for "afterward, Odd Henderson let me alone," Buddy recalls.

But the object of the story lies much deeper than the alleviation of Buddy's problems with Odd Henderson. "The whole family (there were ten of them, not counting Dad Henderson, who was a bootlegger and usually in jail, all scrunched together in a four-room house next door to a Negro church) was a shiftless, surly bunch, every one of them ready to do you a bad turn; Odd wasn't the worst of the lot, and brother, that is *saying* something." The story makes use of the somewhat outmoded philosophy of determinism to some extent, for Odd himself is depicted as "a skinny, freckled scarecrow in sweaty cast-off overalls that would have been a humiliation to a chain-gang convict," and the conditions of his environment shape his behavior. As Miss Sook puts it, "this boy can't help acting ugly; he doesn't know any different. All those Henderson children have had it hard."

There is much more to her understanding of the Hendersons: at the end of the story, Miss Sook puts her arm around Buddy's shoulder. "There's just this I want to say, Buddy. Two wrongs never made a right. It was wrong of him to take the cameo. But we don't know why he took it. Maybe he never meant to keep it. Whatever his reason, it can't be calculated. Which is why what you did was much worse: you *planned* to humiliate him. It was deliberate. Now listen to me, Buddy: there is only one unpardonable sin—*deliberate cruelty*. All else can be forgiven. That, never. Do you understand me, Buddy?" Miss Sook's words are central to an understanding of *The Thanksgiving Visitor*.

Furthermore, they have far-reaching implications in Capote's
system of values because they clarify some of the perplexities of
evil and its origins that occur in the pages of *In Cold Blood*. In
that book, the murderers Richard Hickock and Perry Smith are,
in a very real sense, prisoners of their pathological childhood. As
a consequence, their crimes are rendered understandable, but
not forgivable.

In its narrative style, *The Thanksgiving Visitor* is one of the
more quotable of Truman Capote's stories because of his
occasional flashes of linguistic brilliance. As Miss Armstrong (a
strong-armed schoolteacher) beats Buddy's hands for having
called Odd a "sonafabitch," Odd looks on with "a small citric
smile." Somewhat later, Buddy comments that "my mind
wandered through a maze as melancholy as the wet twilight."
Observing Odd's ears, Buddy regards them as "a pair of eye-
catchers, like Alfalfa's in the *Our Gang* comedy pictures," and as
he watches Odd urinate, he sees him "unbuttoning his trousers
and letting go with a forceful splash [as] he whistled along,
jaunty as a jaybird in a field of sunflowers."

Capote's stories are frequently invested with certain gothic
elements. In a fight with a tomboy named Ann "Jumbo"
Finchburg, Odd suffers "a broken thumb, plus scratch scars that
will stay with him to the day they shut his coffin." And of the
"Henderson breed," he writes that they might well "gouge the
gold out of a dead man's teeth." While Odd's act of thievery is
being exposed at the Thanksgiving dinner, he "seemed calm as a
corpse," and as Buddy fantasizes about his own funeral, he says it
would be "worth it to hear the human wails and Queenie's howls
as my coffin was lowered into cemetery depths."

III   *"House of Flowers"*

"House of Flowers" (1950) must be considered among the
lighter tales, although like those it is not altogether made up of
sweetness and light. The central character is a comely prostitute
named Ottilie who in the early part of the narrative is in the
employ of a "spinsterish, smooth-looking invalid" woman who
operates the Champs Elysées bordello in Port-au-Prince from an
upstairs room. Ottilie, notwithstanding her pleasant and engaging manner, has not passed an easy life. Her mother has died, her
father has returned to France, and Ottilie herself has been left in

the custody of "a rough peasant family, the sons of whom had each at a young age lain with her in some green and shadowy place." At fourteen, she had walked two days and a night to Port-au-Prince carrying what was originally a ten-pound sack of grain. To ease the strain, she has allowed the grain to run out gradually until there was little of it remaining at her arrival. "A jolly nice man" has dried the girl's tears and has taken her "to see his cousin," the proprietress of the Champs Elysées, where she has become the only employee under thirty, and easily "the most talked about girl on the road."

At a cockfight she meets Royal Bonaparte who spirits her away as his wife to his house of flowers. Convinced by a Houngan in the hills above town that love has come to her at last, she has also been led to believe that if she clutches a wild bee in her bare hand, and if the bee does not sting, then love is real. Although this test has disproven her love for a bordello customer named Mr. Jamison, it indicates the genuineness of her attachment to Royal. Her main problem after five months of marriage to Royal is not so much that he has been spending great amounts of time at cafes and cockfights, but that she has been tormented by her mother-in-law, a more than petulant woman known as Old Bonaparte. The old woman not only spies on Ottilie's love-making, but also harasses her by placing the severed head of a yellow cat on Ottilie's sewing basket. Later, Old Bonaparte places other things in the basket, such as a green snake, spiders, a lizard, and a buzzard's breast. Ottilie retaliates by incorporating such morsels as these in her cooking for the old woman. She drops the cat head into a boiling pot and serves Old Bonaparte a soup that turns out to be "surprisingly tasty." But when Ottilie reveals her culinary practices to her mother-in-law, the shock is so extreme that the woman dies by nightfall. Ottilie, however, imagines at night that "Old Bonaparte was dead but not gone," and she confesses to her husband that she has served the old woman such things as snake stew. Royal concludes that she must be punished by being tied to a tree for an entire day without food or water as "the goat Juno and the chickens [gather] to stare at her humiliation."

Still tied to the tree, Ottilie thinks she is dreaming when Baby and Rosita, two of her former associates from the Champs Elysée, arrive in an automobile hired by Jamison, and attempt to bring Ottilie back to Port-au-Prince where her absence has

caused trade at the bordello to fall sharply. They untie the girl
and drain a bottle of rum in "a toast to old times, and those to
be." Finally, Ottilie insists on being retied so that, as she explains,
"no bee is ever going to sting me." Thus, rather than being
"dead," as the invalid proprietress has said of Ottilie, Ottilie is
not only alive, but in love. "Chewing eucalyptus leaves to
sweeten her breath," Ottilie throws "her arms akimbo, [lets] her
neck go limp, [and lolls] her eyes far back into their sockets [so
that] seen from a distance it would look as though she had come
to some violent, pitiful end." This, she concludes, will give Royal
"a good scare."

In spite of the story's sometimes unsavory and unfunny
elements, the narrative is not only witty, but curiously innocent
and romantic, inasmuch as Ottilie possesses a childlike mentality
and lives a life (in spite of her shady past) that seems idyllic.
Ottilie's story is fundamentally consistent with the pattern
established by other Capote protagonists, for she is a virtual
stranger whose influence is strongly felt by those with whom she
comes into contact. At seventeen, her precocity at handling
people and situations invites a comparison with (for example)
Lily Jane Bobbit of "Children on Their Brithdays." Both
characters prove to be virtually irresistible to those around
them, and it is precisely this irresistibility that distinguishes some
of Capote's other key short-story protagonists such as Appleseed
("Jug of Silver") and Tico Feo ("A Diamond Guitar"). Moreover,
Capote's three longer narratives (*Other Voices, Other Rooms;*
Breakfast at Tiffany's; and *The Grass Harp*) have as central
characters individuals with considerable personal appeal. Gone
are such unattractive and audibly introspective personalities as
Mrs. Miller ("Miriam"), Walter Ranny ("Shut a Final Door"), and
Sylvia ("Master Misery").

CHAPTER 3

Three Novel-Romances

CAPOTE's longer narratives are, of course, open to different avenues of interpretation. One such avenue is as an expression of his own life experience, inasmuch as all of the longer pieces are not without their clear autobiographic side. But from a somewhat different point of view, the pieces are an outgrowth of his short fiction in both style and content. Of the three extended narratives, the first two—*Other Voices, Other Rooms* (1948) and *The Grass Harp* (1951)—rely upon the American South as setting. The third, *Breakfast at Tiffany's* (1958), is set in New York, the scene of about half of his short stories. The tenor of the three books is such that they are all well within the province of the "novel-romance," for as Ihab Hassan has written, all attempt successfully "to engage reality without being realistic."[1]

Other clear similarities exist between the longer and the shorter fiction. Capote's preferences in protagonists—usually young and invariably eccentric—prevail in a world that is both comic and sinister at the same time: innocent in some respects, corrupt in others. Withal, it can hardly be questioned that in the short stories lie the literary grist out of which the longer pieces were conceived and written. There is, moreover, a relationship between theme, image, and symbol that exists among all three books.

I *Other Voices, Other Rooms*

Professor William L. Nance has remarked that *Other Voices, Other Rooms* "is an almost unbelievably intricate book," [2] a view emphatically not shared by Alberto Moravia who saw it as "extremely simple in scheme and plot."[3] It is intricate enough, in any case, to demand at least a repeated reading in order to look beneath the subtle but deceptively simple narrative that Capote published at the age of twenty-four. The overt action of the novel seems perhaps simple enough at a first glance: thirteen-year-old Joel Harrison Knox has come from New Orleans to Noon City en route to Skully's Landing where he expects to be reunited with his father, Ed Sansom, who has been missing from Joel's life for the past twelve years. Joel's divorced mother has just died, and he is responding to an invitation, ostensibly written by Sansom and conveyed to Joel's aunt and guardian Ellen Kendall in New Orleans. Sansom's letter proclaims that he is once again prepared to assume his "paternal duties, forsaken, lo, these many years," and that he can now provide Joel with "a beautiful home, healthful food, and a cultured atmosphere." Ellen Kendall has urged Joel to depart for Skully's Landing on the condition that he has the option of returning to his original home, should he become discontent. Joel senses, however, that his departure is a relief to her.

In Noon City Joel arranges a ride on a turpentine truck bound for Paradise Chapel, where he will need to make still other transportation arrangements to Skully's Landing; he completes the trip on a buggy driven by the seemingly ancient Jesus Fever, a Negro with a curved back and a face "like a black withered apple." The twelve-year-old twins Florabel and Idabel Thompkins hop aboard Jesus Fever's wagon also. Florabel has a girlish temperament but Idabel is so much a tomboy that she reminds Joel of "a beefy little roughneck" he had known in New Orleans.

Joel arrives in Skully's Landing asleep and is ushered sleepily to his quarters where he awakens the following morning in an "immense four-poster." From his bed he catches a first glimpse of his father's wife, Miss Amy, ominously killing a bluejay. There is a knock at his door, but instead of his father, it is Miss Amy, who gives him an oblique welcome, and explains that the house has neither electricity nor plumbing. She also tells Joel that "Cousin" Randolph, a "poor child" who suffers from asthma, was born in the bed in which Joel had slept, and that Angela Lee, Randolph's mother, had died there.

Joel makes repeated inquiry about his father, but he receives no information. He makes the acquaintance of Jesus Fever's niece Missouri, a young black servant girl who answers to the name "Zoo," and who tells Joel that at the age of fourteen "this mean buzzard name of Keg . . . did a crime to me and landed hisself in the chain gang." The crime, it turns out, was that Keg (Zoo's husband) succeeded in cutting her throat. Zoo is convinced that "Papadaddy [Jesus Fever] gonna outlive Methusaleh," but even so, "when he gone" she is "aimin' to light out for Washington D. C., or Boston, Coneckikut" so that she can fulfill her ambition of seeing snow. But although Joel and Zoo become friends, she admonishes him, "don't never ax me nothin bout Mister Sansom. Miss Amy the only one take care of him. Ax her."

Bored and confused, Joel decides to revert to a childhood diversion he calls Blackmail, "a kind of peeping-tom game he had known in New Orleans, where he had witnessed such baffling things as "a young girl waltzing stark naked to victrola music" and "two grown men standing in an ugly little room kissing each other." He looks up at the yellow walls of the house and wonders which of the top floor windows belong to him, his father, Cousin Randolph, and it is at this moment that he sees a "queer lady . . . holding aside the curtains . . . smiling and nodding at him, as if in greeting or approval." The queer "woman" is actually Randolph in sexual disguise, although Joel is not yet aware of "her" identity. When Joel asks Randolph about the woman at the window, he receives no answer. Instead, Randolph prefers to talk about the marriage of Keg and Zoo, and of Keg's cutting her throat. Joel asks once again "when am I going to see my dad," but Randolph's only answer is "when you are quite settled." Joel does, however, succeed in finding out about the Cloud Hotel, once "located in these very woods," and owned by Mrs. Jimmy Bob Cloud who, after a series of tragic deaths associated with the hotel, "went to St. Louis, rented herself a room, poured kerosene all over the bed, lay down and struck a match."

Joel discovers later on that it was Randolph, and not Edward Sansom, who had written Joel's letter of invitation to Ellen Kendall. But in a still more important discovery, he at least sees his father, who appears to him only as "a shaved head lying with invalid looseness on unsanitary pillows." Sansom is paralyzed and helpless, and his only means of communication is to drop tennis balls on the floor to attract attention. Following the realization of his father's condition, Joel accepts an invitation from the masculine Idabel to go fishing, where in turn she invites him to bathe naked in a creek. When Joel hesitates, she spits between

her fingers and informs him that "what you've got in your
britches is no news to me," and when he attempts to kiss her a
few minutes later, she attacks him by pulling his hair and causing
him to "cut his buttocks" in the scuffle that ensues.

With Randolph again, Joel learns the background of the whole
set of bizarre circumstances into which he has been plunged.
Randolph had been living in Europe for two years, copying
paintings in museums, living with a woman named Dolores, and in
love with a prize fighter named Pepe Alvarez, who was managed
at that time by Ed Sansom. Apparently because of complications
arising out of Sansom's "owning Pepe," Randolph has sent a
bullet through Sansom's back, and sent him falling down a flight
of stairs. In his agony, Sansom called for Joel, and meanwhile,
Amy has come from Skully's Landing to play the role of nurse
and wife. "Thus," says Randolph, "we all came back to the
Landing; Amy's idea, and the only solution, for he would never
be well again." These events, coincident with his mother's death,
account for the position in which Joel now finds himself.

Jesus Fever dies and is placed in an unmarked grave beneath a
moon tree. Zoo embarks on foot for points North, but soon
returns, tragically, after having been raped by a white man and
his four accomplices. Joel goes with Idabel to see the black
hermit Little Sunshine who still lives in the dilapidated remains
of the Cloud Hotel. On the way to the hotel, Joel kills a snake
with Jesus Fever's war sword, but the two youngsters never
complete their trip to Little Sunshine's. Instead, they come to a
carnival where they meet the midget Miss Wisteria, a twenty-
five-year-old "girl" who has "gold sausage curls" and a
"pennyflute voice." Joel rides a Ferris wheel with her, at which
time she runs her hand between his legs. A rainstorm interrupts
the scene, blackening the carnival lights.

Joel falls ill, runs a fever, and dreams a vivid scenario involving
all the persons who have played a part in his life. Upon his
recovery, Randolph takes him to see Little Sunshine who,
Randolph says, "wants to see us." But Little Sunshine had not, in
fact, been expecting the pair, nor is he pleased to see them when
they arrive. Randolph and Joel tie the mule, John Brown, to a
spittoon and enter the Cloud Hotel where, shortly, the mule
follows them upstairs. Soon, however, the animal "lunged,
splintering [off of] the balcony's rail" and remained suspended

by the neck in death. Randolph and Little Sunshine are by this time impossibly drunk. When morning dawns, it is "like a clean slate for any future." In an act of revelation, Joel climbs a tree and begins to see, among other things, the essence of his own identity: "I am me . . . I am Joel, we are the same people." He sees too that Randolph is "more paralyzed than Mr. Sansom." He then guides Randolph back to Scully's Landing where, in the book's final paragraph, he sees the queer woman once again in Randolph's window: "She beckoned to him . . . and he knew he must go," but he pauses momentarily to look back "at the boy he had left behind."

Other Voices, Other Rooms is, of course, open to various kinds of explanation, but probably the most imposing of these is as an initiation story. Capote makes it very clear during the development of the novel that his Joel Knox is one more on the lengthy list of essentially innocent American boy-men who appear so often in the pages of American literature from Mark Twain's Huckleberry Finn to J. D. Salinger's Holden Caulfield. Like Nathaniel Hawthorne's Robin in "My Kinsman, Major Molineux," Joel Knox is a naive young man who has left his home in search of better things: an improved living circumstance, and a father who will pilot him through his difficult adolescent years. The development of *Other Voices, Other Rooms* is therefore partly to be measured in terms of Joel's gradual shedding of childhood innocence and his progressive movement toward maturity and a sense of personal identity.

When first seen in the novel, Joel appears "too pretty, too delicate and fair skinned," with an aura of "girlish tenderness" about him. Just as Robin carries a cudgel with him as a talisman, and as Holden Caulfield bears a red hunter's cap, Joel brings with him the wedding trip valise once used by his grandfather Major Knox, "a prominent figure in the Civil War." He bears also the spurious letter attributed to Edward R. Sansom with its promises of a better life for Joel. But the longer Joel travels, the more strange and perilous his journey becomes. His new Panama hat is stolen in the Biloxi railway depot, and after that, the bus to Paradise Chapel "had run three hot, sweaty hours behind schedule." Upon his arrival at Skully's Landing, Amy refers to him as a "poor child," and, like Hawthorne's Robin, Joel is referred to as a "shrewd youth." Still later, Miss Amy calls Joel "a

wise, thrifty boy." Longing to come of age, Joel writes his friend
Sammy Silverstein back in New Orleans that "out here a person
old as us is a grown up person." In the woods with the tomboy
Idabel, however, Joel's hoped-for maturity fails him. She tells
him a bawdy joke: (". . . so the farmer said: 'Sure she's a pretty
baby; oughta be, after having been strained through a silk
handkerchief,' ") but Joel fails to comprehend. "Skip it, son,"
Idabel replies. "You're too young."

When Randolph delicately informs him of the "grotesque
quadruplets" (Randolph, Dolores, Pepe, and Sansom), and of the
dangerous love quadrangle that has developed, Joel is taught a
new lesson in life. Randolph tells him that "any love is natural
and beautiful that lies within a person's nature, and that "only
hypocrites would hold a man responsible for what he
loves. . . ." About to give Joel Papadaddy's sword, Zoo hesitates,
for fear that Joel is still "not man enough for to own it." But the
gift is bestowed anyway, and Joel uses it to kill the snake that
threatens Idabel and himself during their journey to find Little
Sunshine at the Cloud Hotel. Along with those other initiates in
American literature, Joel decides that he is going to return to a
less threatening way of life he had once known, but he learns
that he can't go home again. At the carnival he notes that even
that "darling little girl" Miss Wisteria weeps because "little boys
must grow tall." He knows too that his Aunt Ellen was relieved to
see him go, and that in spite of her offer to have him back for
holidays (or for good, if he were discontent), she has, in fact,
"never answered his letters." It is in his understanding of such
circumstances as these that Joel accepts his destiny and moves in
the direction of Randolph, the "she" who beckons to him from a
window on the novel's final page. By this time Joel has indeed
left the boy in him behind.

The novel can, of course, be read in other ways. As in James
Joyce's *Ulysses*, there is the son quite openly in search of a father.
Here, Joel's discovery of his father is an ironic, even ludicrous,
letdown; for Joel no sooner comes to know his father (to the
extent that this debilitated figure can be known) than he resolves
to leave him and run off with Idabel. Toward the beginning of
the book, Capote forthrightly underscores young Joel's ostensible "mission" by stating that "he was trying to locate his father,
that was the long and short of it." On his arrival at Skully's
Landing, Joel wonders how he should at last greet the father he

has never known: "And what should he say: hellow, Dad, Father, Mr. Sansom? Howdyado, hello? Hug, or shake hands, or kiss?" Surveying the "impressive oak doors," Joel wonders later "which of them, if opened, might lead to his father." Fantasizing, Joel tells one of his numerous lies when he writes Sammy Silverstein that "you would like my dad," when in reality Joel has never seen him. He realizes later, still not having "met" his father, that "here no father claimed him." But as Robin meets his kinsman Molineux in tar and feathers, Joel eventually finds Ed Sansom ("poor Eddie, absolutely helpless") to be scarcely a human image. He later regrets ever having seen Ed Sansom, and feels a sense of guilt. Sansom, he thinks, "was not his father," but instead "nobody but a pair of crazy eyes." It is on the occasion of his abortive decision to leave the Landing that he places Sansom's hand against his own cheek and acknowledges the blood kinship between them, whispering "my only father."

Joel's initiatory experiences in the novel are also connected to his "identity" problems, as Capote makes quite clear. "Somewhere along the line," the narrative reads, "he'd been played a mean trick. Only he didn't know who or what to blame. He felt separated, without identity, a stone-boy mounted on a rotted stump. . . ." But at the end of the book when Joel scales a tree, he goes "right to the top," spreading his arms to "claim the world" and proclaim loudly "I am me." There can be no doubt that he has discovered himself and has, in a kind of Joycean epiphany, managed to see, for the first time, the meaning of his world and his destined place in it. His comprehension of these crucial matters comes, symbolically as well as literally, through his journey from New Orleans to Skully's Landing—a peregrination into his own deeper consciousness—which, like the journey undertaken in Joseph Conrad's *Heart of Darkness,* leads into dark, psychic penetration.

Other Voices, Other Rooms is less a novel than it is a gothic romance: brooding, sinister, mysterious, inward-reaching, lyrical, and shadowy. The only sense of reality in it is psychological realism. The book is also a fine specimen of southern regional fiction, conveying as it does the flavor of backwoods life with its "steaming . . . fried eggs and grits, sopping rich with sausage gravy," its overt racism (expressed, but not condoned), its sense of historical heritage (as stated, for example, in the tale of "a fiendish Yankee bandit who rode a silver-grey horse and wore a

velvet cloak stained scarlet with the blood of southern woman-
hood"). Capote, however, once denied the book's sense of place:
"I don't think that *Other Voices, Other Rooms* can be called a
southern novel . . . everything in it has double meanings—it
could as well have been set in Timbuctu or Brooklyn, except for
certain physical descriptions."[4]

Part of the intricacy of the book is Capote's ingenious and
varied use of certain leitmotifs and image patterns. Perhaps
central among these is the consciousness of death and dying, as
intimated in the name "Skully." Not only has Joel's mother died
just prior to the time the narrative begins, but her passing is the
first of a series; Jesus Fever soon dies, as does his mule, John
Brown, that Joel witnesses hanging from the balcony of the
Cloud Hotel: "swinging in mid-air, his big lamplike eyes, lit by
torch's blaze, were golden with death's impossible face, the
figure in the fire." Joel learns too, of the Creole boy who, in 1893,
"having taken a dare to dive into the lake from a hundred foot
oak, crushed his head like a shell between two sunken logs," and
of the gambler who swam out into the same body of water and
never returned. He is aware also of Mrs. Jimmy Bob Cloud who
had immolated herself in St. Louis. The flash of Zoo's gold tooth
reminds Joel of the neon sign heralding "R. R. Oliver's Funeral
Estb." where his mother's body had been taken. "At thirteen," in
fact, "Joel was nearer a knowledge of death than in any year to
come."

As in his shorter fiction, Capote was again attracted by the
grotesqueness he recognized in life, a grotesqueness that appears
often in the course of Joel Knox's education. On first seeing Jesus
Fever slumped atop his wagon, Joel notices the face that looks to
him like a black withered apple and the "sickle-curved posture
that made him look as though his back were broken." There are
other suggestions of grotesqueness, as well. Miss Amy, Joel
observes, has "a vague suggestion of a mustache fuzzing her
upper lip." Idabel claims later on that she used to shave
Randolph's late mother Angela Lee. Later, at the interrupted
carnival scene, however, Joel and Idabel pay ten cents to view a
stuffed chicken with four legs, as well as a "two headed baby
floating in a glass tank like a green octopus." They also encounter
The Duck Boy who, with webbed fingers, opens his shirt "to
reveal a white feathery chest." The midget Miss Wisteria,
dressed in purple silk, sings songs and recites poems through

"rouged, Kewpie-doll lips." She has also a "pale, enameled face" and "hands [that] flitted so about that they seemed to have a separate life of their own." *Other Voices, Other Rooms* is not limited to such prospects as these, for the entire milieu of Skully's Landing is fraught with grotesque distortion. Even at the beginning, Sam Radcliffe, driver of the turpentine truck, finds Joel himself offensive because "he had his notions of what a 'real' boy should be like, and this kid somehow offended them." Joel's appearance and manner, however, are scarcely any match for Randolph's appearances in feminine disguise.

Capote makes extensive use of other images besides grotesqueness, one of these being the image of heat and fire. It is, for example, a "sizzling day in June" when Joel Knox appears in Paradise Chapel on his way to Noon City. After his arrival there, he makes connections with Jesus Fever (who later succumbs to the fever that Joel seems to have contracted near the end of the book). At Scully's Landing, Joel learns from Miss Amy that the dining room, music room, library, and porch have all been destroyed by fire sometime in the past. Still later, he hears about Mrs. Jimmy Bob Cloud who has voluntarily set fire to herself, and about Zoo's having been raped on her way to Washington, D.C., and having been tortured by a lit cigar driven into her navel. With Randolph at Little Sunshine's place in the Cloud Hotel the whole scene is illuminated by firelight.

There are a number of references to the sun, as suggested vaguely in the name "Sansom" and directly in the name "Little Sunshine." At the conclusion of the book, Joel looks skyward and sees images in the clouds. When they pass, he sees also that for him "Mr. Sansom was the sun. He looked down." Earlier he has recalled reading a textbook that informed him "that the earth at one time was probably a white hot sphere, like the sun."

Such heat imagery finds its counterpoint in the chilliness of cold soft drinks, beer, and watermelon. Just prior to his death, Jesus Fever suffers from chills that prompt him to cry out, "How come you let me freeze this away? Fix the fire, child, it's colder'n a well-bottom." Coldness, however, is mostly to be associated with death, and Joel's not infrequent references to snow, as Professor Nance has pointed out, are to be identified with Joel's late mother.[5] That mental association is made reasonably clear in Joel's apocryphal story told to Zoo: "We were lost in the mountains, Mother and me, and snow, tons and tons of it, was

piling up all around us. And we lived in an ice-cold cave for a
solid week, and we kept slapping each other to stay awake: if you
fall asleep in snow, chances are you'll never see the light of day
again."

Capote's concern with animal imagery, however, is as apparent as his concern with images of heat and frigidity. Back in
Paradise Chapel, Miss Roberta, proprietress of R. V. Lacey's
Princely Palace, has "long ape-like arms that were covered with
dark fuzz." At "home" in Skully's Landing, Joel is aware of the
sinister "Judas vine [that] snaked up" the white fluted columns
of the house, while "a yellow tabby cat was sharpening its
claws." Still later, Joel makes the acquaintance of Zoo, the black
woman who informs him of Randolph's liking for dead birds, "the
kinds with pretty feathers." Joel gradually becomes conscious of
the animal life around him: the mules, chicken hawks, lizards,
snakes, hunting dogs, the "big Persian cat" that "sucked away all
[the] breath" of a black infant, the buzzards, ants, and
butterflies that inhabit the mysterious world of Skully's Landing.

There are still other motifs and images that weave the fabric
of the book together. The bullet that Joel Knox steals from Sam
Radcliff during the ride from Paradise Chapel to Noon City
reappears in Joel's feverish dream near the end of the narrative.
The Dr. Pepper and NEHI advertising signs that Joel sees on
Paradise Chapel Highway, as well as the inscription on Idabel's
shirt ("DRINK COCA-COLA") are echoed in the carnival scene
when Joel rushes to ask Miss Wisteria if she might not join him
and Idabel for a "sodapop." And the valise that Joel carries, the
one that his grandfather had "used on his wedding trip around
the world" recalls Randolph's later description of the "honey-
moon" of Keg and Zoo which has ended in his cutting her throat.
Furthermore, the story of the rape and murder of the three
"exquisite sisters" by "a fiendish Yankee bandit," prefigures
Zoo's rape and torture late in the narrative.

Particularly imposing are Capote's knife images that appear
throughout the text. On one occasion, for example, Idabel
brandishes a jacknife with "a thin vicious blade" before Joel's
eyes, while she comments threateningly, "I could kill somebody,
couldn't I?" as she stabs murderously into the side of a
watermelon. There is perhaps an ironic outcome to Joel's prayer
which asks God for "a knife with seven blades," for later Zoo
gives Jesus Fever's sword to Joel ("This here was Papadaddy's

proudest thing") which he straps to his waist and uses eventually
to kill a snake. Joel is, of course, aware of Keg's knife attack on
Zoo, but he is also aware of certain inevitabilities in human life
later on when he notes that (in the case of Miss Wisteria) "there
would always be this journey through dying rooms until some
lovely day she found her hidden one, the smiter with the knife."
   That *Other Voices, Other Rooms* is heavily autobiographic is
perhaps clear enough to preclude any precise documentation.
Involving, as it does, a young man's search for a home, a father,
and a sense of identity, the book is created out of the patterns
that prevailed in Capote's early personal history, although not
necessarily to the letter. Although the book might conceivably
be looked upon as an exercise in Capote's quest for self-
understanding, that approach to the narrative is beyond the
purview of this study. In 1956, Capote remarked that "last
summer I read my novel *Other Voices, Other Rooms* for the first
time since it was published eight years ago, and it was quite as
though I were reading something by a stranger. The truth is, I am
a stranger to that book; the person who wrote it seems to have so
little in common with my present self."[6] Evidently because of the
book's very controversial reception (as noted in Chapter 1) and
the extent to which its author had invested himself in its pages,
Capote seemed to want the whole episode in his career put well
behind him.

II   The Grass Harp

   Again in *The Grass Harp,* Capote constructed a southern tale
around a boy whose parents are deceased and who, as a
consequence, goes to live with relatives. The relatives this time
are two somewhat eccentric maiden sisters, Verena and Dolly
Talbo. *The Grass Harp* is a great deal more elemental and witty
than *Other Voices, Other Rooms,* and much less gothic in tone.
The protagonist is the boy Collin Fenwick, to some extent
another Capote self-portrait, eleven years of age when the story
opens. His mother has died, and soon after his father, a seller of
Frigidaires, has been fatally injured in an automobile accident.
The older sister, Dolly, is Collin's favorite, and the two of them
retire to the woods so that they can discover the natural ingredients necessary to concoct the dropsy remedy that Dolly
prepares, bottles, and sells. But the younger sister, Verena, has

an obsession with money, and is "the richest person in town" because of the drugstore, the drygoods store, the filling station, the grocery, and the office building that she owns. "The earning of it," says Collin, "had nòt made her an easy woman." Verena, Dolly, and Collin are cared for by a black woman named Catherine Creek who resembles Zoo in *Other Voices, Other Rooms,* and who claims to be an Indian, although she is, in fact, "dark as the angels of Africa." Catherine refers to Dolly as "Dollylove," and to Verena as "That One."

When Dolly begins to earn enough from the manufacture of her dropsy remedy to pay income taxes, Verena begins to take a heightened interest in Dolly's enterprise. And when Collin reaches the age of sixteen, Verena embarks on a buying trip to Chicago and returns two weeks later with an enigmatic individual named Dr. Morris Ritz, "that little Jew" who "wore bow ties and sharp, jazzy suits," and who, according to Collin, "might have been a tap dancer or a soda jerk." At a dinner on Talbo Lane attended by Verena, Morris Ritz, Dolly, and Fenwick, Verena and Morris reveal the medicine bottles they have had printed, which read "Gipsy Queen Dropsy Cure." They also reveal their intention to apply to Washington for a copyright on the labels and a patent on the medicine. Dolly objects: "It won't do: because you haven't any right, Verena. Nor you, sir." Dolly is unaware, however, that Verena and Dr. Ritz are preparing to restore an old factory, and that Verena has given Ritz ten thousand dollars to furnish it with the machinery necessary to manufacture the medicine in marketable quantity.

Understandably unhappy, Dolly proposes that she, Catherine, and Collin venture out to a house built in a China tree some distance from Talbo Lane. Once situated in their arboreal home, they are joined by others as time goes on. The first to find and join them is a contemporary of Collin's named Riley Henderson, a fatherless son of a criminally insane mother. Verena, meanwhile, having found a note left by Dolly, goes to Sheriff Junius Candle and requests a search party to locate the three missing persons. From their tree house, the inhabitants look down to see "a distinguished party" approaching that includes Harvard-educated Judge Charlie Cool, the Reverend and Mrs. Buster, Mrs. Mary Wheeler, and Junius Candle himself with "a pistol flapping on his hip." Ordered by the preacher's wife to come down out of the tree, Dolly responds by asking Mrs. Buster to "consider a moment . . . and . . . realize that we are nearer to God than you—by several yards." Following that line of argument, Judge Cool says to Reverend Buster that perhaps "the Lord told these people to go live in a tree; you'll admit, at least, that He never told you to drag them out. . . ." Following this, the judge himself joins the tree party, whereupon Collin remarks that "it was the judge who had most found his place in the tree."

On a later occasion, Sheriff Candle and his men return with a warrant of arrest signed by Verena who has accused them of theft. The three sheriff's deputies ("Big Eddie Stover was legally born a bastard; the other two made the grade on their own") begin to drag Catherine and slap her. Collin hits Eddie Stover in the face with a big catfish, while Catherine elbows and butts her way through the others, and is finally arrested for having struck Mrs. Buster with a Mason jar. It then develops that "Dr." Morris Ritz has suddenly left town, taking with him the contents of Verena's safe—twelve thousand dollars in negotiable bonds and more than eleven hundred dollars in cash. "But even that," Collin says, "was not half his loot."

A travelling family of evangelists, consisting of a woman and her fifteen children, comes to town and begins to promote one of their number, a twelve-year-old boy who wears steel-rimmed glasses and a ten-gallon hat, and looks, consequently, "like a walking mushroom." The homemade sign that the family brings with it reads "Let Little Homer Honey Lasso Your Soul For The Lord." The pathetic troupe come looking for Dolly Talbo, who eventually feeds the entire crew and gives them money. It is Reverend Buster, meanwhile, who applies to the sheriff for an injunction preventing Little Homer Honey from conducting any religious meetings, but the child does so anyway. People "who never dropped a dime in Buster's collection plate" now find themselves hanging dollar bills on "God's Washline," although the money is confiscated by "that puke-face Buster and what's-his-name, the sheriff: thinks he's King Kong."

A short time after their departure from the China tree, Dolly falls ill of the walking pneumonia and eventually dies of a stroke. Riley Henderson survives a bullet wound in the shoulder inflicted by Eddie Stover, and gets married. Collin serves as his best man, and lingers around the town a while "winning free beers on the pinball machine" but at last decides to pursue a degree in law. In the end, Collin strolls out into the Septemberburnished fields that had once surrounded the tree house. "I wanted then," says Collin, "for the Judge to hear what Dolly had told me: that it was a grass harp, gathering, telling, a harp of voices remembering a story. We listened."

As is true with *Other Voices, Other Rooms,* there are a number of points of view from which *The Grass Harp* can be examined to critical advantage. Reduced to its simplest terms, the book depicts the contending forces of conformity and social orthodoxy versus freedom and self-expression. The characters who best typify these differences in approach to living are Verena, who chases wealth; and Dolly, the older sister, who chases dreams. The remaining characters fall in to either of two categories; with Verena are Morris Ritz, the Reverend and Mrs. Buster, Mrs. Mary Wheeler, Sheriff Candle, and his deputies. With Dolly are the protagonist Collin Fenwick, Judge Charlie Cool, Catherine Creek, Riley Henderson, Sister Ida and her fifteen offspring ("Seems somehow I can't get on without another life kicking under my heart: feel so sluggish otherwise"). The contending that goes on in the book, over what are fundamentally questions of social conformity and self-reliance, is weighted in favor of the free-wheeling eccentrics and innocents who follow the way of Dolly Talbo. Consequently, the author's sympathies, predictably enough, are on the side of those who pursue their dreams: "A man who doesn't dream is like a man who doesn't sweat: he stores up a lot of poison" Judge Charlie Cool assures Verena, and his remark, as much as any single remark in the book, identifies its central theme. Earlier, Cool has referred to Dolly, Catherine, Riley, Collin, and himself as "five fools in a tree," but, he says, they are "free to find out who [they] truly are." If the five are not totally successful at unravelling the problem of self-recognition, they at least succeed in gaining some perspective on the world that lies below their tree house, a world which is by all odds less rational than their own.

The Grass Harp has other similarities with *Other Voices, Other Rooms,* for here is another local color story that makes much of the southern setting and its cultural aspects: diet, humor, a sense of place, and of history. Collin Fenwick, like Joel Knox, moves in the direction of self-knowledge and self-understanding which is achieved through a series of seriocomic incidents. Just as Joel Knox has triumphantly proclaimed his self-awareness from the heights of a tree, so too does Collin Fenwick come to terms with himself in a tree. Beyond the outward similarities, many of the leitmotifs are similar. There is, for example, some of the same kind of sexual reversal as in *Other Voices, Other Rooms*. The rumor once spread by Collin's father, "that Verena was a morphodyte," may have been exaggerated, but there are suggestions of her lack of sexual identity. In years past she has formed an attachment to Maudie Laura Murphy who worked in the local post office and who, to Verena's grief, ran away with a liquor salesman. Collin describes Verena as being "like a lone man," and Dolly discloses later that Verena was given to pipe-smoking. Verena eventually admits to Collin that she had loved Morris Ritz, but "not in a womanly way." And yet one of the last things that Collin says of Verena is that in her last years she has "grown feminine."

The preoccupation with death that had prevailed in *Other Voices, Other Rooms*, continues also in *The Grass Harp*. One of the first things to which the reader's attention is directed is the town graveyard containing not only Collin's mother and father, but twenty or so of his kinfolk. When Collin speaks of Carrie Wells, a schoolteacher who had toured Europe, he is reminded that the only things connecting his town with Europe are "the graves of soldierboys." Verena herself has expressed a desire to erect an imposing mausoleum to accommodate all of the Talbo family, and Judge Cool recalls with vividness his wife's dying in his arms. When Maud Riordan contemplates a Halloween party, she urges Collin to appear with "a skeleton voice." Judge Cool, when he vacates the home he had shared with his sons and their wives, rents a room at Miss Bell's boarding house which had only lately been transformed into a funeral parlor.

Another motif which ties the narrative together is the act of theft, a motif present in both *Other Voices, Other Rooms* and *Breakfast at Tiffany's* where the protagonist in each instance has inclinations toward petty thievery. But in *The Grass Harp* the idea of theft is emphasized heavily. Riley Henderson's uncle Horace Holton, it turns out, has been gradually draining the money belonging to his sister Rose. And when the treehouse party departs the house on Talbo Lane, "Catherine bragged that she'd robbed the pantry of everything, leaving not even a biscuit for That One's breakfast." Later, Verena swears out a warrant for the arrest of Catherine, Collin, and Dolly, on the grounds that they have "stolen property belonging to her." The only authentic

theft in the novel, however, is Morris Ritz's cleaning-out of
Verena's safe, although the sheriff's seizure of Sister Ida's revival
meeting receipts seems tantamount to outright theft, as well.
Verena herself, however, would have stolen Dolly's dropsy
formula, if given the opportunity.

Capote uses the imagery of fish in various ingenious ways in
the novel. Collin, at one point, recalls having kept tropical fish:
"devils they were; ate each other up." Catherine, however,
cherishes her goldfish that "fanned their tails through the portals
of the coral castle" in their bowl. Riley Henderson, according to
Collin, was both a good carpenter and a good fisherman. At one
point, Collin suggests to Catherine that they abandon their tree
and live aboard a houseboat owned by a man who makes his
living "by catching catfish," but she declines the suggestion and
insists upon living on land "where the Lord intended us."
Somewhat later, Judge Cool suggests that the tree-dwellers
"should taste my fried catfish sometime," and he recalls having
caught a trout in his bare hand, just as Collin catches a huge
catfish in the same manner. Up in their China tree, the
inhabitants experience a driving rainstorm so severe that "fish
could have swum through the air."

There is also the repetition of a kind of noose-imagery at
certain points in *The Grass Harp.* Chapter Two, for example,
opens in the woods when Riley Henderson comes into view, "and
around his neck there hung a garland of bleeding squirrels."
Collin himself has been hung similarly by Catherine earlier: "At
fourteen," he recalls, "I was not much bigger than Biddy Skinner,
and people told how he'd had offers from a circus." To remedy
Collin's growth deficiency, Catherine pulls at his arms, legs, and
head "as though it were an apple latched to an unyielding
bough." When Charlie Cool first appears at the China tree, he
unloosens from his vest a gold watch and chain, "then lassoed the
chain to a strong twig above his head; it hung like a Christmas
ornament." On an earlier occasion, Verena berates her sister for
her lack of enthusiasm over Morris Ritz's coming to dinner: "I'd
appreciate it if you's hold up your head: it makes me dizzy,
hanging like that." When Sister Ida and her fifteen assorted
offspring arrive in town, it is her "Little Homer Honey" who will
"Lasso Your Soul For The Lord." And in the midst of the
controversy between Reverend Buster, the sheriff, and the
occupants of the tree-dwelling, it is also Little Homer who does

indeed lasso Reverend Buster, but not for the Lord. Little Homer's rope "dangled like a snake, the wide noose open as a pair of jaws, then fell, with an expert snap, around the neck of Reverend Buster, whose strangling outcry Little Homer stifled by giving the rope a mighty tug." Buster, "loose-limbed as a puppet," makes his way off the premises with the aid of several persons as Little Homer calls after him, "Hey, hand me back my rope!"

The Grass Harp is as much in the province of the romance as *Other Voices, Other Rooms*. To borrow the definition cited by Professor Hugh Holman, the romance "differs from the novel in being more freely the product of the author's imagination than the product of an effort to represent the actual world with verisimilitude."[7] In *The Grass Harp* the house built in a China tree, as well as the attic of the Talbo house (from which Collin looks thoughtfully down) are as removed from life on the bare soil as the book's overall removal from the starkness of unvarnished reality. The book itself is partly an illustration of the desirability of adhering to one's private, inner nature rather than yielding to the often hypocritical orthodoxy symbolized, for example, by the Reverend and Mrs. Buster. In his advocacy of adhering to one's inner dictates, Judge Cool says it best: "all private worlds are best, they are never vulgar places."

The quality of Capote's witty prose style is a point of emphasis in itself, quite apart from his use of theme and idea. Catherine's kitchen in the Talbo house, Collin says, is "warm as a cow's tongue." Sheriff Candle has fists "hard and hairy as coconuts." Elsewhere, Capote makes hilarious use of the outrageous and unexpected incident. Observing Riley Henderson urinate over a hill of red ants, Collin is "insulted" when Riley "switched around and peed on my shoe." Toward the end of the book, the reader is introduced to "the twice widowed Mamie Canfield" whose specialty is the early identification of pregnant women from the porch of her boardinghouse-funeral parlor: "Why waste money on a doctor?" one anonymous character is said to have asked his wife. "Just trot yourself past Miss Bell's: Mamie Canfield, she'll let the world know soon enough whether you is or ain't."

Unlike the generally critical reception of *Other Voices, Other Rooms*, the consensus of critical reaction to *The Grass Harp* was positive. Gene Baro, writing for the *New York Herald Tribune Book Review*, for example, proclaimed that "Truman Capote's literary stature seems now beyond question. His second novel, 'The Grass Harp,' supplements the undeniable achievement of 'Other Voices, Other Rooms.' Indeed, the present volume exhibits the maturing and mellowing of one of America's best young writers."[8] Oliver La Farge's review in the *Saturday Review of Literature* read, in part, "It is a real pleasure to see a young author coming along who possesses a change of pace; so many writers of all ages tend to carve eternally off the same joint, even after the meat has grown cold and dry, or even after there is nothing left but scraps. Variety within the broad range of his genre on the part of a writer as able as Truman Capote is something to welcome with cheers."[9]

III   Breakfast at Tiffany's

No writer ever decisively breaks with the thematic and stylistic patterns of his work established over a period of years. *Breakfast at Tiffany's,* which appeared in 1958, seven years after the appearance of *The Grass Harp,* is not inconsistent with the kind of fiction Capote had been writing earlier. *Breakfast at Tiffany's* is a very chic, character-centered novella which is as frothy as it is enigmatic. Narrated in the first person, the tale is a personal story of one who relates the bizarre, somewhat fragmented incidents in the life of Holly Golightly to himself.

In technique, Capote drew upon some of the better features of his talent as a writer, relying as he did on elements of wit, irony of situation and language, lyricism, precision of feeling achieved through selectivity of detail, and an all-but-inexhaustible sense of satire. Capote's handling of wit is facilitated by the fact that Holly Golightly is one who quite literally lives by her wits. When, for example, she elects to evade an investigation of her supposed complicity in New York Mafia racketeering by an escape to Brazil, she makes a final outrageous request of the narrator: "Call up the *Times,* or whatever you call, and get a list of the fifty richest men in Brazil. I'm *not* kidding. The fifty richest: regardless of race or color." But the narrator disapproves of her plans to bolt the country and engage in Brazilian fortune-hunting while the police are looking for her in New York. "If they catch you jumping bail, they'll throw away the key. Even if you get away with it, you'll never be able to come home." But Holly has an answer for everything: "Well, so, tough titty. Anyway, home is where you feel at home. I'm still looking."

The book is virtually centered on a series of startling disclosures. Holly turns out to be not the "Miss Holiday Golightly, of the Boston Golightlys" as reported in a recent newspaper gossip column, but the former Lulamae Barnes, the runaway wife of Doc Golightly, a horse doctor from near Tulip, Texas. Golightly himself appears midway in the story: ". . . I bought myself a ticket on the Greyhound [from Texas]. Lulamae belongs home with her husband and churren." Holly, who has a proclivity for chewing her hair and for acts of petty theft ("I'd steal two bits off a dead man's eyes if I thought it would contribute to the day's enjoyment . . ."), has been hired by a defrocked priest named Mr. Oliver O'Shaughnessy (who impersonates a lawyer) to visit convicted Mafia figure Sally (Salvatore) Tomato in jail every Thursday. At a meeting in Hamburg Heaven, O'Shaughnessy has asked Holly "how I'd like to cheer up a lonely old man, [and] at the same time pick up a hundred a week . . . Well, I couldn't say no: it was too romantic." The whole idea, of which Holly seems incredulously unaware, is that Sally Tomato provides her with "verbally coded messages" having ostensibly to do with the weather, but which in reality are designed to permit Tomato (through Holly and O'Shaughnessy) "to keep first-hand control of a world-wide narcotics syndicate with outposts in Mexico, Cuba, Sicily, Tangier, Tehran and Dakar." If Holly is not entirely aware of her own acts, their meaning, and consequence, neither is the narrator, or for that matter, the reader.

The narrator himself relies on a number of sources for information about Holly. In addition to his attempts at sorting through her own oblique remarks, he talks to her conspicuously unattractive male friends, has conversations with bartenders, and looks at disclosures in newspapers. In spite of his inevitable inconclusiveness after this kind of investigation, he says, "I became . . . rather an authority on [her]." In a particularly telling series of details, he relates his having rifled through the discarded odds and ends that make up her personal trash-basket. "I discovered," he says, ". . . that her regular reading consisted of tabloids and travel folders and astrological charts; that she smoked an esoteric cigarette called Picayunes; survived on cottage cheese and melba toast; that her vari-colored hair was somewhat self-induced. The same source made it evident that she received V-letters by the bale. They were always torn into strips like bookmarks. I used occassionally to pluck myself a bookmark in passing. *Remember* and *miss you* and *rain* and *please write* and *damn* and *goddamn* were the words that recurred most often on these slips; those, and *lonesome* and *love.*"

These discarded artifacts of Holly's past life are projected into the larger fabric of the novella. It is in the city tabloids that her alleged social and criminal activities are exposed. The travel folders are emblematic of her restless spirit, and of the kind of life implied on the engraved card fitted into her apartment mailbox: *Miss Holiday Golightly, Traveling.* The astrological charts reveal something of the antirational, perverse, and unpredictable character of her life. They also confirm Holly's later remark that she has abandoned horoscopes, as she says, because they are a "bore." The Picayune cigarettes contain a hint about her somewhat mysterious and veiled southern origins. Her diet of cottage cheese and melba toast in part explains "all her chic thinness" and her "almost breakfast-cereal air of health" as evidenced by "a flat little bottom." Her hair coloring contains some indication of the deception with which her past and present life are clouded. But it is the V-letters written by service men that provide the best insight into her lonely and loveless existence. Torn as they are into slips that serve for bookmarks, the letters serve as a record of her unfulfilled, romantic dreams.

Holly, for all of the rumors and conjecture that surround her, is another example of an all-but-unassailable innocence. The narrator remembers her first as being ageless: "anywhere between sixteen and thirty." In reality, she is not yet nineteen, with "a face beyond childhood, yet this side of belonging to a woman." Her age and innocence are reminiscent of Kay in Capote's early story "A Tree of Night," who carries with her a green Western guitar into which she pours a glass of unwanted gin. Walking toward Joe Bell's bar, the narrator of *Breakfast at Tiffany's* bears with him what little Holly has left behind after her hurried departure for Brazil, and as he walks, Holly's abandoned guitar fills with rainwater. The innocence that Holly shares with Kay is in a way similar to the easy candor and outspoken bluntness observable in Miss Lily Jane Bobbit in "Children on Their Birthdays." The inscrutable D. J. in "The Headless Hawk" (another New York story) has in common with Holly a thoroughly unpredictable pattern of social behavior, along with a history of psychiatric treatment. What unites these characters is a paradoxically fortunate inability to shed the color and fantasy of childhood. As a consequence, they share a certain immunity from the tragic reality of life, an immunity characteristic of the prostitute Ottilie in the story "House of Flowers."

In the end, Holly makes good on her flight to Brazil, and then moves on to Argentina where she passes into oblivion. The last thing known about her destiny comes from an unlikely source (the Japanese photographer I. Y. Yunioshi), a former resident in Holly's brownstone in the East Seventies, who shows bartender Joe Bell three photographs taken in Africa of a black man "displaying in his hands an odd wood sculpture" which passes for "the spit-image of Holly Golightly." Yunioshi's investigations indicate that Holly, accompanied by two white men, had found their way to Tococul, "a village in the tangles of nowhere" where the two men had fallen victim to a fever and where Holly had allegedly "shared the woodcarver's mat." This is the last thing known about her. "All I hope," says Joe Bell, "I hope she's rich. She must be rich. You got to be rich to go mucking around in Africa." The only troublesome item that Holly (who wanted to "wake up some morning and have breakfast at Tiffany's") has left in New York is a cat with no name. Concluding two weeks of "after-work roaming through . . . Spanish Harlem streets," the narrator finds the nameless animal "flanked by potted plants and framed by clean lace curtains, . . . seated in the window of a warm-looking room." Says the narrator, "I wondered what his name was, for I was certain he had one now, certain he'd arrived somewhere he belonged. African hut or whatever, I hope Holly has too."

Like the previous two novel-romances, *Breakfast at Tiffany's* can be read variously. Probably the most salient reading of the book is as a celebration of innocence and as a mirthful example of the short-circuiting of an essentially tragic and evil world, as symbolized by the wicked, ugly prospect of Manhattan and its inhabitants that forms the background for Lulamae, once the wife of Doc Golightly of Tulip, Texas. Although it is scarcely emphasized, the narrator's exposure to Holly has apparently been another step in his education as a writer of prose fiction. Toward the beginning of the book she asks him, quite undiplomatically, if he is a *real* writer. "It depends on what you mean by real," is his evasive response. "Well, darling, does anybody buy what you write?" she asks. "Not yet," is his reply. Later, he reads her a short story he has written; he notices that she fidgets, and that he "did not seem to have her interest." In the course of the book he manages to place some of his writing in a quarterly magazine, and on the final page of the book he discloses that he has sold two stories. It becomes gradually clear that it is Holly herself who has given him a subject worthy of writing about: herself.

Breakfast at Tiffany's shares with most of Capote's other fiction a concern for people who are liberated from the more commonplace moorings of social and cultural life, and who are scarcely concerned with such things as family relationships and middle class notions of respectability. To read *Breakfast at Tiffany's* is to become aware that the novelette itself is in part a deliberate affront to middle class respectability, consistency, dependability, and to the whole cluster of values that form the Protestant Ethic. When the narrator warns Holly that if she jumps bail, she will never again be able to come home, it impresses her not at all. Holly, like so many disengaged Capote characters, is decidedly outside the normally construed notions of value and reality. Holly prefers to be "natural" rather than "normal," and her manner of coping with the world makes her engaging not only to her author, but to the reader. She represents a certain independence of mind and freshness in her approach to manners and morals, albeit *Breakfast at Tiffany's* is not a particularly morally conscious book.

The consensus of reviewer's attitudes toward *Breakfast at Tiffany's* was almost uniformly high, and although no single review was noteworthy for its critical insight into the book, each of them found much to praise and virtually nothing to criticize negatively. Paul Levine, in the *Georgia Review,* made what is perhaps the most memorable comment about Capote and his new book when he remarked, "Like good whiskey (and unlike many of our one-shot novelists) Capote seems to improve with age."[10] Levine, like other followers of Capote, was by this time able to know what to expect from the author, and had identified a refinement in Capote's skill as a fiction writer.

Among the tendencies that might have ben expected, for example, was a certain retrospective point of view in his fiction, and this point of view was again to prevail: "I am always drawn back to places where I have lived, the houses and neighborhoods," the narrator of *Breakfast at Tiffany's* remarks, ". . . there is a brownstone in the East Seventies where, during the early years of the war, I had my first New York apartment." That the narrator is once again to be closely identified with the author, perhaps goes without saying, for the narrator is, at this juncture in his career, a struggling writer of fiction whose work is mostly unsold and therefore unpublished. That Holly Golightly has provided him with something vital to write about means that she has inadvertantly been a major force in his life and in his prospects as a writer. For the narrator, the end of the novelette is just the beginning. Holly is somewhere in Africa (perhaps). Sally Tomato has succumbed to heart failure at Sing Sing. Holly's former friends, the Trawlers, are now in the midst of divorce proceedings. But the narrator has managed to sell two more short stories and has vacated his brownstone apartment "because it was haunted." The ending of *Breakfast at Tiffany's* is not significantly different from the ending of *The Grass Harp* where the real center of the story is the impact it has on its narrator-protagonist: "a grass harp, gathering, telling, a harp of voices remembering a story."

CHAPTER 4

The Shift to Reportage

I'VE always had the theory that reportage is the great unexplored art form," Capote once remarked to an interviewer.[1] Certainly he, more than any other established American writer, has done more with the immense possibilities inherent in what might be called "creative reporting." The essence of this creative reportage is to set down a continuum of factual information in such a way that it carries a fictive quality to its presentation. It involves, therefore, the imposing of artistic order and arrangement over a body of information that, while lending itself to systematic narration, nevertheless requires a sense of structure and coherence.

Capote, whose development as a fiction writer had included ample enough attention to artistic design and coherence, advanced by stages to reportorial pieces like those contained in *Local Color* (1950) to the greater sophistication of longer and more complex experiments such as "The Muses Are Heard" (1956), "The Duke in His Domain," and finally to his truly monumental undertaking in "the non-fiction novel," *In Cold Blood* (1965). All of these efforts were published originally in the pages of *The New Yorker*. "I think reportage has helped me," Capote said. "I think it freed many things inside of me—this opportunity to work with real people. . . . It has freed or unlocked something inside of me that now makes it possible for me to return to fiction with the greater ability to use a far greater range of characters."[2] Obviously, Capote brought to bear on his reporting the imaginative faculty necessary for the writing of high quality fiction. "One of the reasons I wanted to do reportage," he said once, "was to prove that I could apply my style to the realities of journalism. But I believe my fictional method is equally detached—emotionality makes me lose writing control: I have to exhaust the emotion before I feel

94

clinical enough to analyze and project it, and as far as I'm concerned that's one of the laws of achieving true technique. If my fiction seems more personal it is because it depends on the artist's personal and revealing area: his imagination."[3] Like fiction, distinguished reporting depends partly upon the selection and organization of relevant detail. For as Granville Hicks has remarked (with specific reference to *In Cold Blood*), "It is not the gathering of data that counts, impressive as that is, but the organization of this mass of material."[4]

Capote began his experiments in the art of reporting with relatively slight pieces (with fewer problems in organization), and progressed to longer, infinitely more ambitious undertakings. In retrospect, it would appear that until the Clutter murders in Kansas occurred, Capote was not only gaining experience at creative reporting, but also somehow waiting for the ideal incident to report *about*. The gruesome murders took place in the autumn of 1959, and they offered an infinitely broader appeal to readers than Capote's travel sketches of Haiti, or for that matter his extended interview with actor Marlon Brando. Still, the Clutter affair had very broad public interest for other than morbid reasons. The Clutters were more than respectable upper-middle-class individuals with whom a huge public could easily identify. In addition, there seemed to be a "market" for close scrutiny of the homicidal criminal mentality, a scrutiny in which Capote was to excel. His selection of the Clutter case was fortunate in more ways than one. *The New Yorker* is said to have paid $70,000 for printing each of the four sections in serial form, and in addition, the New American Library allegedly paid more than $700,000 for permission to reprint. The book's motion picture rights, which were sold to Columbia Pictures, were supposedly worth nearly a million dollars.[5] But the events that led up to this literary pot of gold have their origins in Capote's early attempts at imaginative reporting that began with *Local Color*.

I   Local Color

The collection consists of nine impressionistic travel-vignettes which had appeared originally in periodicals between 1946 and 1950. Each of the nine pieces dwells upon a particular Capote

haunt: "New Orleans" (1946), "New York" (1946), "Brooklyn"
(1946), "Hollywood" (1947), "Haiti" (1948), "To Europe"
(1948), "Tangier" (1950), and finally "A Ride Through Spain"
(1950). All of the sketches are, in fact, varied exercises in local
color writing, as the general title accurately denotes, and
Capote's objective in each of the nine pieces was to capture the
flavor of the specific location, and achieve a sense of "place."
New Orleans, he says for example, "like every southern town is a
city of soft-drink signs; the streets of forlorn neighborhoods are
paved with Coca-Cola caps, and after the rain, they glint in the
dust like lost dimes." In New Orleans the author once called
upon a certain elderly and aristocratic friend referred to only as
"Miss Y" who "is like the piano in her parlor—elegant, but a little
out of tune."

In "Tangier" he speaks of Estelle, a beautiful girl who walks
"like a rope unwinding," and of unvarying breakfasts consisting
of "a bowl of fried octopus and a bottle of Pernod." With a similar expressiveness in "A Ride Through Spain" Capote wrote of an
extended train journey in which the "seats . . . sagged like the
jowls of a bulldog." In his Hollywood essay he described the
sensation of approaching Los Angeles by air; it is similar, he
imagines, to "crossing the surface of the moon: prehistoric
shapes, looming in stone ripples and corroded, leer upward, and
paleozoic fish swim in shadowy pools between desert mountains:
burned and frozen, there is no living thing, only rock that was
once a bird, bones that are sand, ferns turned to fiery stone."

What Capote offered the reader in *Local Color* was less an
embellishment of reality than a greater insight into it, and what
the sketches reveal most is the author's extraordinary powers of
perception. Except that they are essays, they seem only slightly
removed from the same powers of observation applied to the
writing of fiction. The nine parts of *Local Color* are, from
another point of view, exercises in critical observation which are
not yet developed and unified into sustained pieces of reportage
such as *The Muses Are Heard* and, of course, *In Cold Blood.* From
yet another point of view, the sections that make up *Local Color*
are in the moribund tradition of the travel book, in that they are
prompted not only by a sense of place, but of situation. The *Local
Color* essays were, for Capote's aesthetic and intellectual set of
mind, comparatively slight efforts at imaginatively colored
journalistic flights intended for those who read more for
linguistic delight than for didacticism. In *The Muses Are Heard,*

however, Capote seemed somewhat more interested in situation than in setting, and his account of a trip behind the Iron Curtain was concerned less with local customs and points of historic significance than with what is usually called "human interest" elements. It was designed, in other words, for a more varied reading audience. Capote's success at reporting seemed to increase in proportion to his growing ability to make "real life" appear to be fictitious; indeed, he himself apparently saw little difference between his skill at writing fiction and his skill at reporting "life": "Actually, I don't consider the style of this book, 'The Muses Are Heard,' as markedly different from my fictional style," he once remarked.[6]

II   The Muses Are Heard

The New Yorker carried *The Muses Are Heard* in two of its 1956 issues, after which it was reprinted by Random House that same year. The two-part account of Capote's trip to Leningrad in 1955 with the American cast of *Porgy and Bess* and an assortment of other personalities is, not surprisingly, written in *The New Yorker* manner: engaging, smart, witty, and brilliant in its powers of subtle observation. The first of the two parts ("When the Cannons Are Silent") treats the preliminaries for the Russian performance of the play by introducing the company principals during a "briefing" in a West Berlin rehearsal hall, and then by describing the arduous rail trip (consisting of three days and nights) to Leningrad. The second installment ("The Muses Are Heard") deals with the five days of rehearsal that culminate in the performance of December 26.

Although the concern of the book is more with situation than with place, *The Muses Are Heard* can be regarded as another travel book, far more elaborately developed than the isolated pieces in *Local Color* had been. This time Capote seemed more absorbed in the contrast in culture that he observed, and he illuminated some differences between American manners and those in the U.S.S.R. Another point of his emphasis was with character, so much so that *The Muses Are Heard* became a veritable mosaic of personality sketches, centering on such people as columnist Leonard Lyons, Mrs. Ira Gershwin, co-producer and director Robert Breen, actors Bruce Jackson, Helen Thigpen, and numerous others.

Some of these character portraits, indeed, were to be among

the more memorable ones in the Capote gallery of portraits written over the years. When, for example, actor Earl Bruce Jackson is introduced, Capote describes him as "tall and lean, a live-wire with slanting eyes and a saturnine face. He affects a chin goatee, and his hands are radiant with rings, diamonds, sapphires and rubies. We shook hands. 'Peace, brother, peace. That's the word . . .'" But when Mrs. Gershwin arrives on the scene, Capote pictures her as "a small and fragile woman devoted to diamonds [who] wears them, quite a few, at both breakfast and dinner. She has sun-streaked hair and a heart-shaped face. The flighty fragments of her conversation delivered in a girlish voice that rushes along in an unsecretive whisper, are pasted together with terms of endearment."

Written, as it was, in the midst of the Eisenhower anti-Communism fervor of the middle 1950s, anything approaching an amiable cultural exchange of this kind would have been regarded by some as daring and revolutionary at best, subversive at worst. At the time of writing, Capote was not unaware of the supposed inferiority of Russian manners and political values. Upon seeing their first authentic Russians (two Soviet "train officers" and some sleeping car attendants), Capote's American travelling companions "stare . . . as though amazed, and rather peeved, to discover Russians had two eyes correctly located." The political implications of the *Porgy and Bess* tour are never too far removed from Capote's consciousness, for, after all, "the Gershwin opera, when slipped under the dialectical microscope [is] a test tube brimming with the kind of bacteria to which the present Russian regime is most allergic." Capote was aware also that *Porgy and Bess* blatantly "sings out loud that people can be happy with plenty of nothin', an unwelcome message indeed," and that the musical play illustrates that American blacks are "an exploited race at the mercy of ruthless Southern whites, poverty-pinched and segregated in the ghetto of Catfish Row."

In spite of numerous discomforts, inconveniences, and mischances along the way, the play goes on as scheduled, and *The Muses Are Heard* concludes with a series of rave reviews from critics back home who have drawn their conclusions about the Russian performance from reports of the play's reception cabled out of Russia.

Capote was influenced enough by the current anti-Russian feeling in America that he could scarcely draw an engaging portrait of the Russian people in general. He makes much of the somewhat ironic and unpredictable reactions to the play itself, and depicts the Russian people as being not only repressed, but baffling in their attitude toward such matters as art, politics, gastronomy, and humor. He draws the reader's attention to one individual, a Russian with one eye whose age is somewhere between forty and seventy, and whose idea of comedy is to parody Christ on the cross: "Taking a swallow of beer, he would stretch his arms and drop his head. In a moment a trickle of beer came crying out of the gaping redness of his hollow eye socket. His friends at the table thought it was an uproarious stunt."

The Muses Are Heard is itself, at times, an uproarious stunt. Highly readable, honest, witty, and incisive, it provided Capote with the kind of reporting opportunity for which he was looking at that point in his career, and with a chance to put shape and sense into an otherwise unheralded experiment in the arts. The favorable reception of *The Muses Are Heard* was in part a factor that convinced Capote that he might look still more deeply into the creative possibilities of reporting.

III   *"The Duke in His Domain"*

His next excursion into reportage was to deal with what he called "the most banal thing in journalism": an interview with a motion picture star. After Capote sat through an extensive series of interviews with actor Marlon Brando in Japan, he passed another year writing "The Duke in His Domain" which appeared in the November 9, 1957 issue of *The New Yorker*. His portrait of Brando seemed to stress three main artistic objectives. In addition to its being a close-up portrait of the actor himself, it became also an exercise in local color writing and an exquisite display of literary stylistics. As a character sketch, "The Duke in His Domain" placed its emphasis upon Brando's somewhat bizarre mode of living: his tastes in books, foods, friends, actors, and theater. Compressed within the pages of a single essay (and what appeared to be a single interview), "The Duke in His Domain" provided an astute and comprehensive vision of Brando's temperament and world view.

At the time of the interviews, Brando was engaged in the making of the motion picture *Sayonara*, and the occasion was to give rise to Brando's musings on life and art. "The only reason I'm here," Brando told Capote, "is that I don't have the moral courage to turn down the money." Of the deceased actor James Dean, Brando comments, "He had an *idée fixe* about me. Whatever I did he did. He was always trying to get close to me." Capote has by this time learned elsewhere that "Marlon always turns against what he's been working on," and consequently his views toward the earlier picture *On the Waterfront* are perhaps understandable, if ironic: "The first time I saw *Waterfront*, in a projection room . . . I thought it was so terrible I walked out. . . ." The conversation then turns to more personal matters, during which time Brando admits that his "main trouble" is his "inability to love anyone." This problem notwithstanding, Brando then comments at length on his circle of friends: "I'm all *they* have. A lot of them, you see, are people who don't fit anywhere; they're not accepted, they've been hurt, crippled one way or another. But I want to help them, and they can focus on me; I'm the duke. Sort of the duke of my domain."

Capote's interest in, and penchant for, local color writing is this time focused on the postwar Japanese scene, this time with precision of insight and genuine feeling for this alien culture. As he keeps his interview appointment with Brando at the Miyoko Hotel in Kyoto, he notes that "most Japanese girls giggle," and that the maid on Brando's fourth floor "was no exception." He continues, "Hilarity and attempts to suppress it, pinked her cheeks (unlike the Chinese, the Japanese complexion more often than not has considerable color), shook her plump peony-and-pansy-kimonoed figure." Of the Japanese rice wine *sake*, Capote remarks that although some connoisseurs claim to have the ability to distinguish "variations in taste and quality in over fifty brands," to him and to other novices, it "seems to have been brewed in some vat . . . pleasant at first, cloying afterward, and not likely to echo in your head unless it is devoured by the quart, a habit many of Japan's *bons vivants* have adopted." Back out on Kyoto's streets in the middle of the night following the interview, Capote notes "a neighborhood of curving roofs, the dark façades of aristocratic houses fashioned from silky wood yet austere, northern, as secret-looking as any stone Siena palace. How brilliant they made the street lamp appear, and the doorway lanterns casting keen kimono colors—pink and orange, lemon and red." An hour's drive from Kyoto, Capote describes Nara, "a postcard town set in a show-place park," and an example of "the apotheosis of the Japanese genius for hypnotizing nature into unnatural behavior." Here in this "great shrine-infested park" are "swarms of fish, speckled and scarlet carp, fat, thick as trout who allow their snouts to be tickled."

One of the differences between *Local Color, The Muses Are Heard,* and "The Duke in His Domain" is that Capote himself played a participant's role in the first two, whereas in "The Duke in His Domain" he remained much more in the background. In the Brando interview he is scarcely more than a provocateur, one to whom the interviewee responds. This tendency to remove himself from the role of participant in his own reportage is no where better illustrated than in the text of *In Cold Blood* where he remained strictly outside of the grim narrative; he was, in other words, detached but not unmoved by what he had unearthed about the Clutter murders. In both "The Duke in His Domain" and *In Cold Blood* Capote essentially marshalled facts, incidents, and details that he allowed to speak for themselves. For all of his personal involvements in Kyoto and Kansas, there are virtually no private responses to any of the thousands of details reported there.

In spite of Capote's disinterestedness in the circumstances surrounding the Clutter case, *In Cold Blood* is not without its moral dimensions, whereas his earlier reporting had not, even at a distance, dealt with anything approaching a moral issue. But the moral problems raised in the text of *In Cold Blood* go far beyond the violation of the Sixth Commandment, for aside from the fact that a ghastly crime has taken place, Capote extends the question of culpability far beyond the killers themselves to include the social and psychological forces that have shaped their lives and given rise to their misdeeds.

IV   In Cold Blood

Capote's preparations for the writing of *In Cold Blood* began long before the Clutter tragedy had occurred. It was around 1953, Capote said, that "I began to train myself, for the purpose of this sort of book, to transcribe conversation without using a tape-recorder. I did it by having a friend read passages from a book, and then later I'd write them down to see how close I could come to the original. I had a natural faculty for it, but after doing these exercises for a year and a half, for a couple of hours a day, I could get within 95 per cent of absolute accuracy, which is as close as you need."[7] Capote's technique of listening carefully and later transcribing conversations and details without the use of a recording device, undoubtedly helped to facilitate interviews with individuals who were wary of having their voices committed to tape.

Always the inveterate devourer of newspapers, Capote, (now at the age of thirty-five) was attracted to a minor news item in a November, 1959 issue of The New York Times. "I found this very small headline that read 'Eisenhower Appointee Murdered.' The victim was a rancher in western Kansas, a wheat grower who had been an Eisenhower appointee to the Farm Credit Bureau. He, his wife, and two of their children had been murdered, and it was a complete mystery. They had no idea of who had done it or why, but the story struck me with tremendous force. I suddenly realized that perhaps a crime, after all, would be the ideal subject matter for the massive job of reportage I wanted to do. I would have a wide range of characters, and, most importantly, it would be timeless. I knew it would take me five years, perhaps eight or ten years, to do this, and I couldn't work on some ephemeral, momentary thing. It had to be an event related to permanent emotions in people."[8]

With an impulsiveness not untypical of him, Capote left New York for the Kansas plains with such haste that he reached his destination in time to witness the mass funeral of the murder victims. His companion on the trip was his lifelong friend, the novelist Harper Lee. "We traveled by train to St. Louis, changed trains and went to Manhattan, Kansas, where we got off to consult Dr. James McCain, president of Mr. Clutter's [the victim's] alma mater, Kansas State University. Dr. McCain, a gracious man, seemed a little nonplussed by our interest in the case, but he gave us letters of introduction to several people in western Kansas. We rented a car and drove some 400 miles to Garden City," Capote recalled later.[9]

Here began a nearly endless series of interviews and correspondence with virtually anybody who had anything to do with the murdered Clutter family and the mystery that surrounded the killings. For Capote, the investment in energy and time was enormous. "I did months of comparative research on murder, murderers, the criminal mentality, and I interviewed quite a number of murderers—solely to give me a perspective on these two boys [the Clutter family murderers Perry Smith and Richard Hickock who were eventually convicted of, and executed for, the crime].[10] Between 1959 and 1965 Capote did little other than research, write, and revise his manuscript of the Clutter case. The outcome of his labors was *In Cold Blood*, the astonishingly well-documented account of the murder, what led up to it, and its aftermath. Capote's research for the book amounted to some six thousand pages of interviews, including extensive testimony from the killers themselves.

His conversations with Perry Edward Smith and Richard Eugene Hickock spanned a period of five years, during which time the killers became "the two people he knew most intimately in the world."[11] When the night of the executions by hanging arrived, Capote accompanied the pair to the gallows. "Going back to Kansas to watch the execution was unquestionably the most intense emotional experience of my life," he told Shana Alexander of *Life* magazine, "but the boys wanted me there, so of course I had no choice. I spent the entire two days before the execution throwing up in my motel room . . . but somehow when the time came I got myself together and went there and spoke to them quite rationally, I think, and at the hanging I stood as close to them as I am to you now. When it was over I started to cry and couldn't stop. . . . They finally had to call a doctor to the prison to give me something and get me on the plane home."[12] Smith (thirty-six years old) and Hickock (thirty-three years old) were hanged at the Kansas State Penitentiary for Men on April 14, 1965.

A virtually unparalleled triumph in creative reporting, *In Cold Blood* appeared in successive 1965 issues of *The New Yorker* between September 25 and October 16. After six years of the most intensive and thorough research imaginable, the book was to illustrate a great many things, not the least of which is Capote's remarkable talent as raconteur. From another point of view, *In Cold Blood* is an extended illustration of the immense possibilities of local color writing, supremely orchestrated in its progression and tone. Divided into four sections, the book begins by establishing the character of the town of Holcomb "on the high wheat plains of western Kansas, a lonesome area that other Kansans call 'out there' " and where "the last seven years have been years of droughtless beneficence." The narrator then closes in on the River Valley Farm of Herbert William Clutter, where he discusses the whole Clutter family soon to be murdered in cold blood by Smith and Hickock.

Once underway with the narrative, Capote alternates his attention between the wholesomeness of the Clutter family (notwithstanding the mother's proclivity toward a vaguely understood mental illness) and the hideous criminality of their eventual slayers. Ultimately, the paths of the two parties converge and culminate in the multiple shotgun murders. The effectiveness of Capote's orchestration can best be illustrated at two points in the book's first section, "The Last to See Them Alive." On the first occasion, five armed intruders appear at the Clutter farm, and although they are finally identified merely as "pheasant hunters from Oklahoma," their appearance at this time is an ominous sign. Herbert Clutter sets about his day's work "unaware that it would be his last." On the second occasion, after the bodies of the four murdered Clutters have been discovered, and after law enforcement officers, friends of the Clutter family, and the press have been summoned to the River Valley Farm, Capote heightens the inconceivable horror of the circumstances by contrapuntally changing the subject for the time being; whereas one subsection ends with the hysterical testimony of one onlooker ("The suffering. The horror. They were dead. A whole family. Gentle. Kindly people, I knew, *murdered.* You have to believe it because it was really true"), the following subsection commences with some ostensibly irrelevant remarks: "Eight non-stop passenger trains hurry through Holcomb every twenty-four hours. Of these, two pick up and deposit mail—an operation that, as the person in charge of it fervently explains, has its tricky side." The subject then turns to Mrs. Sadie Truitt, mail messenger for the town of Holcomb, whose regular workday, this Sunday morning, is interrupted by the sight of two ambulances that cross the railroad tracks and turn toward the Clutter property.

The artistic value of *In Cold Blood* is as much to be found in its illuminating, minute detail as it is in its total impact. Some of these details are more than casually revealing. The Clutter home, for example, is decorated in part by an ominous "liver-colored carpet," a detail that only an inattentive reader is likely to forget. Murderer and ex-convict Perry Smith is described as "no taller than a twelve-year-old child . . . strutting on stunted legs that seemed as grotesquely inadequate to the grown-up bulk they supported, not like a well-built truck driver but like a retired jockey, over-blown and muscle bound." Of Nancy Clutter, one of Smith's four murder victims, the reader is told that at sixteen she had been "the town darling," having distinguished herself as "a straight-A student, the president of her class, a leader in the 4-H program and the Young Methodists League, a skillful rider, and excellent musician (piano, clarinet), [and] an annual winner at the county fair (pastry, preserves, needlework, flower arrangement). . . ." Smith's partner in crime, Richard Hickock, has "imperfectly aligned features" as a result of an automobile collision in 1950, "an accident that left his long-jawed and narrow face tilted, the left side lower than the right, with the result that the lips were slightly aslant, the nose askew, and his eyes not only situated at uneven levels, but of uneven size, the left eye being truly serpentine, with a venomous, sickly-blue squint that although it was voluntarily acquired, seemed nevertheless to warn of sediment at the bottom of his nature." And as the events of the reconstructed crime begin to converge before the reader's eye, he is reminded too that Holcomb is situated in the midst of the "Bible Belt" which Capote describes as "that gospel-haunted strip of American territory in which a man must, if only for business reasons, take his religion with the straightest of faces. . . ."

The second part of *In Cold Blood* ("Persons Unknown") deals with the aftermath of the multiple murders, including the bafflement of the Kansas Bureau of Investigation and other law enforcement agencies about the apparent lack of a plausible motive for the crime. Neither Nancy Clutter nor her mother, it is disclosed, were "sexually molested," and to all appearances, nothing had been stolen from the Clutter home. Capote then describes the mass funeral and the horrid appearance of the four bodies: "the head of each was completely encased in cotton, a swollen cocoon twice the size of an ordinary blow-up balloon, and the cotton, because it had been sprayed with a glossy substance, twinkled like Christmas-tree snow."

Concurrently, he follows the travels of Smith and Hickock through a wild, bad-check-passing spree through Mexico and back again, after which he probes the early life and emotional development of Smith, emphasizing his disjointed and traumatic youth. He concludes by depicting the murderers marching along an all-but-deserted highway in the Mojave desert, singing "The

Battle Hymn of the Republic" to the accompaniment of a
harmonica stolen the day before from a Barstow, California,
variety store.

Part three ("Answer") is the climactic section of the four,
dealing as it does with the eventual apprehension of Hickock and
Smith on the strength of a tip given by a prisoner-acquaintance
of theirs still behind bars. The next to last subsection of part
three may well be the most emotionally stressful piece of writing
in all of modern reporting because it deals with what the reader
has been wanting most to find out about: the precise circumstances of the murders. The intense emotional course of Perry
Smith's account of the crimes flows like the course of the Arizona
highway along which he travels in the custody of detectives. His
confession follows with a description of Smith and Hickock's
entering the unlocked door of the Clutter home, their futile
search for a nonexistent safe, and their awakening of Herbert
Clutter, his wife, and their teen-aged daughter and son. The
victims are tied, and their mouths bound with tape. Clutter and
his son are removed to the basement where the killers cut
Clutter's throat as a preliminary to the shotgun blast to the head.
After his death come those of son Kenyon, daughter Nancy, and
wife Bonnie—all by the same means. In response to a detective's
inquiry about how much money was stolen from the Clutter
family comes the final and ironic reply: "Between forty and fifty
dollars."

There is some question at this point in the narrative about
Capote's guarded feeling and attitude toward Hickock and
Smith. He has by this time devoted considerable time and space
to the grotesque biographic history of both men, and the
implication is that these àtrocities can be explained as the
outcome of a kind of fatal determinism that has worked through
the lives of the killers since the day they were born. Of Perry
Smith, Capote writes, "life had been no bed of roses but pitiful,
and ugly and lonely progress 'toward one mirage and then
another." Of the crime itself, Capote continued, it "was a
psychological accident, virtually an impersonal act; the victims
might just as well have been killed by lightning. Except for one
thing: they had experienced prolonged terror, they had
suffered."

While it is possible, even rational, to see the tragic series of
events described in the pages of *In Cold Blood* as a complex of

cause-and-effect circumstances wherein fate is determined by sheer chance and accident, it is also possible to view the Clutter murders as the logical outcome of sociological and psychological forces that had gained gradual momentum over the years. Capote represents Hickock and Smith as moral perversions of decent men brought about by the poverty, violence, and ill-luck that reached back for at least one generation. The Clutter family, by contrast, is also a product of its environment, except that the family history has been characterized by more positive elements than those that had permanently scarred the lives of the killers.

It is significant that Capote at no time renders a judgment about the criminals. His determined disinterest is maintained for at least two reasons: it is important for the reader to draw his own conclusions about the philosophical-sociological-psychological circumstances of the mass murder, and Capote was determined not to interfere with the reader's judgmental process. He is nonjudgmental also because of his rather thorough understanding of the evolution of the killers' lives. To react with either condemnation or sympathy would seem, in the context of the book, irrelevant to its basic issues: the reasons for the crime and how it could have occurred. Capote is primarily concerned with motivations and circumstances that form an engrossing but inscrutable web of factors that rendered Smith and Hickock moral invalids, psychopathic criminals. It becomes evident that questions of condemnation and sympathy toward the criminals have no real bearing from an objective standpoint.

The fourth and final part of the book ("The Corner") treats the incarceration, multiple legal complications, and eventual death by hanging of the defendants. "The Corner" is of particular interest because of its two methods of documentation. The first of these is a generous portion of the defendants' autobiography, and the second is a pointedly detailed psychiatric report on both the prisoners. Smith, for example, writes of his experience in one of several detention homes to which he was committed as a youth: "I had weak kidneys & wet the bed every night. This was very humiliating to me, but I couldn't control myself. I was very severely beaten by the cottage mistress, who had called me names in front of all the boys. She used to come around at all hours of the night to see if I wet the bed. She would throw back the covers & furiously beat me with a large black leather belt—pull me out of bed by my hair & drag me into the bathroom & throw me in the tub & turn the cold water on & tell me to wash myself and the sheets. Every night was a nightmare. Later on she thought it was very funny to put some kind of ointment on my penis. This was almost unbearable. It burned something terrible. . . ." The psychiatric examiner writes of Hickock, "he shows an unusual pattern of intermittent periods of productive activity followed by patently irresponsible actions" and "he secretly feels inferior to others and sexually inadequate." The report continues, "he is uncomfortable in his relationship to other people, and has a pathological inability to form and hold enduring personal attachments." In summary, the examiner reports, "he shows fairly typical characteristics of what would psychiatrically be called a severe character disorder." Of Perry Smith he comments, "he seems to have grown up without direction, without love, and without every having absorbed any fixed sense of moral values." Documentation such as this inevitably lends heavy and convincing credibility not only to the behavior of the murderers, but also to Capote's narrative itself.

The impact of the book is reinforced, somewhat ironically, by several well-handled digressions, not the least of which is the eerie account of the Clutter estate auction, and by the seemingly unrelated disclosure of the criminal careers of certain death-row companions of Smith and Hickock at the Kansas State Penitentiary in Lansing. Capote writes that, as the auction progresses, "Mr. Clutter's worldly domain dwindled, gradually vanished." He quotes a bystander as saying that the disposal of the family estate was "like a second funeral." But the gallery of rogues awaiting death at the penitentiary reveal through Capote's account of their crimes some sense of the criminal culture out of which Hickock and Smith had evolved their criminality.

Like most good writing, *In Cold Blood* is constructed on a series of ironic elements. One of these elements has been cited earlier: Capote's steadfast resistance to offering any kind of moral judgment on the Clutter affair. But other ironies of a situational sort are present almost without end in the book. Example: as the Clutter family is in the process of being murdered in this otherwise remote farming region of western Kansas, at the same moment, less than a hundred yards from their home lives Alfred Staeklein who, along with his wife, is awake caring for a sick infant. There is also detailed information about the Clutter watchdog Teddy, an otherwise menacing animal whose ferociousness utterly disappears at the sight of a gun. Still other ironic elements include the inscription on Mrs. Clutter's silk bookmark inserted in her Bible which bears the ominous admonition: "Take ye heed, watch and pray: for ye know not when the time is." Capote also discloses Hickock's numerous tattoos, one of which is "the word PEACE accompanied by a cross radiating, in the form of crude strokes, rays of holy light." Shortly before the murder, the Japanese Mrs. Ashida chats with Herbert Clutter. "Just nothing scares you," she remarks. "No matter what happened, you'd talk your way out of it." Later on, the reader learns that Clutter has indeed been unable to talk his way out of his own and his family's impending murder. The reader also learns that Clutter, just prior to his murder and at the age of forty-eight, had signed with New York Life Insurance for a $40,000 policy on himself, "that in the event of death by accidental means, paid double indemnity." The forty or fifty dollars that Smith and Hickock carry away from the murder scene is a consequence of their lack of awareness that Herbert Clutter "was famous for never carrying cash." When Nancy Clutter on the Saturday night of her death, sets out a certain red velveteen dress she has made herself and expects to be wearing to the Methodist church in the morning, the dress becomes instead the one in which she is buried. In the final, single page subsection of part one, the reader encounters Smith and Hickock—some eight hundred miles from the scene of the crime—each asleep. "Perry Smith lay sleeping, with a portable radio [that he had taken from Kenyon Clutter] murmuring beside him" in a cheap hotel room. A short distance away, at the home of his parents, Richard Hickock snores through a television broadcast of a basketball game. Not only is their sedate response to this atrocity ironic, but similar to the response of Feodor Dostoevsky's character Raskolnikov in *Crime and Punishment,* and to Richard Wright's character Bigger Thomas in *Native Son,* both of whom fall into a coma-like sleep following their homicidal acts.

The day after Smith and Hickock are apprehended by the Las Vegas police happens to be the day that Nancy Clutter would have been seventeen. Floyd Wells, the Kansas State Penitentiary convict who won both a parole and a cash reward for his testimony leading to the apprehension of Smith and Hickock, eventually falls into bad times. "At present," Capote writes, "he is a resident of the Mississippi State Prison in Parchman, Mississippi, where he is serving a thirty-year sentence for armed robbery." Once Smith and Hickock are returned to the Finney County Courthouse to await trial, the wife of undersheriff Wendle Meier takes ironic pity on the prisoners by preparing their meals to order. Says she: "I didn't want those fellows going to bed on an empty stomach." Perry Smith's confession about the crime and its victims has, by his own recognition, a heavily ironic side to it. "It wasn't because of anything the Clutters did," he told Capote during a prison interview. "They never hurt me. Like other people. Like people have all my life. Maybe it's just that the Clutters were the ones who had to pay for it." It is strange too, that during the initial trial "the question of whether Hickock or Smith had been the actual executioner of the Clutter family did not arise." As one lawyer representing the accused argues passionately for life imprisonment instead of the death penalty, Capote focuses attention on the inattentiveness of one juror who "as though poisoned by the numerous spring fever yawns weighing in the air [sits] with drugged eyes and jaws so utterly ajar bees could have buzzed in and out." Ironic, too, is the conspicuously lame attempt on the part of Perry Smith's ex-prison chaplain James E. Post to circulate a snapshot reproduction of "a head-and-shoulders portrait of Jesus Christ done in pastel crayon" by the defendant. "Any man who could paint this picture," argues the Kansas State Penitentiary cleric, "can't be one hundred percent bad." After the conviction, with its stipulation of the death penalty, the two prisoners break into a loud laugh, and the initial (but later revised) date set for their execution at the so-called "warehouse" turns out to be "one minute after midnight on Friday, May 13, 1960."

In the final subsection of *In Cold Blood*, and after a number of stays of execution, the moment finally arrives when the pair are to be put to death by hanging. Hickock greets law enforcement agents Roy Church, Clarence Duntz, Harold Nye, and Alvin Dewey—all of them key figures in the Clutter case—by saying "nice to see you," and by offering "his most charming smile." Capote continues, "it was as if he were greeting guests at his own funeral."

These ironic elements are a few of many that characterize the book. Capote, like virtually all writers of stature, views life partly as a pattern of interlocking ironies, and his recognition of this pattern is nowhere more apparent than in the pages of *In Cold Blood*. Moreover, there is a sense in which the events leading up to the murder, the trial, and the execution do not at all form a rational pattern of cause-and-effect relationships. Capote again raises the question of why the innocent are made to suffer, and why on occasions such as the one outlined in the book, men of imagination and intelligence find their powers subverted to evil ends. Finally, the "why" of the Clutter murders is left hanging like the scarecrow dressed in Mrs. Clutter's "weather-faded flowered calico dress " which is left "forlornly dancing in the cold December field."

An important aspect of the book's manner of narration is its reliance upon a contrapuntal technique involving the contrast of short subsections within the four main divisions. The contrasts themselves can be seen in more than one way, as for example contrasts of light and dark, optimistic and tragic, productive and counterproductive. It is clear enough that the generally positive, successful, productive character of the Clutter family contrasts vividly with the essentially negative, unsuccessful and unproductive lives of Perry Smith and Dick Hickock. Hickock himself was aware of this contrast; in the third section of *In Cold Blood* the reader is informed that "envy was constantly with him; the Enemy was anyone who was someone he wanted to be or who had anything he wanted to have." Capote also stresses the contrast between the two men, a contrast that is both physical and temperamental. In the Finney County Jail, Smith is pictured in contrast to his surroundings. "He looked," Capote says, "as lonely and as inappropriate as a seagull in a wheat field." In still another contrast, the "trust in God," that had once "sustained" Mrs. Clutter is pitted against the moral and philosophical waste land of her executioners.

The ending of *In Cold Blood* brings with it enormous changes in tone and situation that contrast with the beginning of the book. The Clutters and their killers are dead. Judge Tate, in whose courtroom the killers were brought to trial, has died of pneumonia. The reader subsequently learns also that "Nancy Clutter's boy friend, young Bobby Rupp [once a murder suspect in the case] had gone and got married." Nancy's close friend Susan Kidwell is now a junior at the University of Kansas where Nancy herself had anticipated studying. The book's ending

comes as close to being an emotional appeal to the audience as
any other place in Capote's lengthy "nonfiction novel," dealing
as it does with what might have been if the whole tragic series of
events had not come to pass.

Considered as a nonfiction novel, *In Cold Blood* contains
woven throughout the text a number of thematic elements that
demand scrutiny. One of these, and possibly the central one,
involves the relationship between "life" and "art." When Capote
made his initial visit to Kansas to attend the Clutter family
funeral and to begin his painstaking and costly research, the
crime did not necessarily have any prospects for a "solution,"
meaning that the outcome of the police investigation, like the
outcome of Capote's own research into the case, was somewhat
blindly and open-endedly undertaken. There is the prevailing
assumption that "life" provides only the raw materials out of
which "art" is fashioned, and that until the artist somehow
modifies, proportions, and rearranges these raw materials, there
can be no art. Part of the experience of reading *In Cold Blood* is
the impression that life has indeed somehow taken on the
balance and proportion of art. Capote had managed to orches-
trate the story of the Clutter murders, not through the distortion
of fact, but by the reordering and proportioning of it. In terms of
focus, the book moves between the activities of the victims, the
criminals, and the law-enforcement people. In terms of time, he
moves without restriction between past and present. Once aware
of the crime, the reader moves back in time to follow the course
of events that led up to it. But while the reader can depend upon
the high degree of accuracy in Capote's documentation, it should
be borne in mind that the selectivity of detail and the particular
points singled out for emphasis are elements left to the discretion
of the artist himself.

It is obvious that *In Cold Blood* transcends the usual limitations
of journalism, partly because of the shape and structure given it
as part of an artistic conception. The subsections of the four main
parts of the book are often cameo essays, each with a statement
of its own. These smaller units of varied tone and emphasis are
then arranged in a montage of artistic forms. Some of these
subsections are memorably finished pieces of work, such as the
one with which the book ends. Here Capote pictures inspector
Alvin Dewey at the Valley View Cemetery tending to the weeds
that had overgrown his father's grave. Dewey chances to meet

Susan Kidwell, who is paying a visit to the four Clutter graves "gathered under a single gray stone." Susan is home temporarily from the university that she and Nancy had anticipated attending together. When Susan departs the scene, the book ends with Dewey's intense recognition that Susan is as Nancy could have been: alive and attractive, graceful and refreshing. He watches her as she disappears down the cemetery path, "a pretty girl in a hurry, her smooth hair swinging, shining—just a young woman as Nancy might have been. Then, starting home, he walked toward the trees, and under them, leaving behind him the big sky, the whisper of wind voices in the wind-bent wheat." This ending, incidentally, and as Professor Nance has pointed out, bears a marked resemblance to the ending of *The Grass Harp* ("a grass harp, gathering, telling, a harp of voices remembering a story").[13]

Among the other thematic sides to the book is a version of what might be called the myth of crime and punishment, wherein most of the book's ability to evoke tension in the reader rests on the emotional effects of a vicious but temporarily unsolved crime. Unlike the more conventional mystery tale such as might have been written by Edgar Allan Poe or Arthur Conan Doyle, Capote has relied on a kind of dramatic irony where the reader is mostly aware of the crime and its perpetrators before anyone in the book is. The reader is, moreover, a silent witness to the murder and to the flight of the killers as they move from points in Mexico to Miami, Florida, to avoid detection and to pursue their vain hopes of a future bonanza.

Capote himself once cited an interpretation of *In Cold Blood* as seen by those of his readers who wrote him their impressions of the book: "About 70 percent of the letters think of the book as a reflection on American life—this collison between the desperate, ruthless, wandering, savage part of American life, and the other, which is insular and safe, more or less."[14] The "collision" he speaks of underscores the fact that the book is constructed partly on strongly contrasting elements, and also that it contains the chance and accidental convergence of forces that Capote feels are a major factor in the determination of human fate.

There is also periodic evidence throughout the book of sexual aberration and its effects, although such detail, not unlike a goodly measure of other kinds of detail, is left to the reader for interpretation. When first seen in the book, Perry Smith is pictured with a guitar and an assortment of roadmaps—the same possessions that Capote's character Tico Feo had with him in the short story "A Diamond Guitar." In both contexts the guitar would appear to function as a feminine image and symbol. Perry Smith, like the fictional Tico, is a dreamer who strums his guitar plaintively and dreams of his personal day of liberation; and whereas "A Diamond Guitar" contained elements of homosexuality, the reader learns that part of what attracts Dick to Perry is that Dick feels "totally masculine" by this association. Somewhat later in the first section of the book, Perry is seen entering their 1949 Chevrolet sedan in the back seat of which is the Gibson guitar and the phallic "instrument" that typifies his companion Dick: "a twelve gauge pump-action shotgun, brand-new, blue-barreled, and with a sportsman's scene of pheasants in flight etched on the stock." Elsewhere in the book Dick addresses Perry as "sugar," "honey," and "baby." Later still, Dick becomes aware of Perry's bed-wetting and his habit of sitting "for hours just sucking his thumb"—all of which causes Dick to regard him as "such a kid." In 1945, the reader is informed, Perry entered a Honolulu tattoo parlor and ordered a "snake-and-dagger applied to his left forearm." Later, in a controversy with his father over a biscuit, Perry went into such a rage that he gripped his father's throat: "My hands . . . I couldn't control them. They wanted to choke him to death." A snapshot made of him during his term in the Merchant Marine is described by Capote as "a pretty-little-boy portrait."

After the murder, in Mexico, the two killers take up with a German named "Otto" and "a 'swish' pair of Negro prizefighters driving a 'swish' lavender Cadillac." Discovered among Perry's property left at a cheap Las Vegas rooming house is "a scrapbook thick with photographs clipped from physical culture magazines (sweaty studies of weight-lifting weight lifters)." When the two chomp on stolen chewing gum, Dick's preference is for the Doublemint, while Perry is partial to the sweeter tasting Juicy Fruit. In Las Vegas, and shortly before their apprehension by police, Dick is weary of his companion, and plans to strike out on his own. Perry's "harmonica, his aches and ills, his superstitions, the weepy, womanly eyes, the nagging, whispering voice" all irritate him. Moreover, Perry was to Dick "like a wife that must be got rid of." As it happens, Perry Smith turns out to be the first male resident of the "ladies cell" after he is brought back to

Finney County to await trial. Once deposited in his cell, he passes the time as best he can. "He found things to do," says Capote, "file his fingernails with an emery board, buff them to a silky pink sheen; comb and comb his lotion-soaked and scented hair. . . ."

Dick Hickock is presented in different terms. Capote discloses in part three of the book that he is "sincerely ashamed" of his habit of "seducing pubescent girls." In the first section of *In Cold Blood*, Hickock recalls his father's having bought him a bicycle: "it was a girl's bike and he changed it over to a boy's." In a document written by Hickock himself the reader learns more about what Capote calls Hickock's "pedophiliac tendencies." Hickock writes, "the main reason I went [to the Clutter home] was not to rob them but to rape the girl." He continues, "I did make some advances toward the Clutter girl when I was there. But Perry never gave me a chance." Still later, Capote quotes Alvin Dewey's remark that Smith allegedly told Hickock that "there wasn't going to be anything like that go on," and that furthermore "Smith told me he had no respect for anyone who didn't control their sexual desires. . . ." .

Capote himself did not apparently think of *In Cold Blood* as espousing a thesis or message. He told Perry Smith that the book "didn't have anything to do with changing the reader's opinion about anything, nor did I have any moral reasons worthy of calling them such—it was just that I had a strictly aesthetic theory about creating a book which could result in a work of art."[15] Indeed, the research, background, and writing of *In Cold Blood* is in some respects a story as interesting as the finished product. Haskel Frankel's account of the making of the book (*Saturday Review*, January 22, 1966) reveals a number of fascinating and profoundly ironic details of Capote's personal adventures in Kansas after the Clutter murders had taken place. "I hate violence," Capote said to Frankel, but nonetheless Capote had been attracted to *The New York Times* article treating the Clutter murders: "It was sort of as though one had been sitting for a long time watching for a certain kind of bird—if you were a bird watcher—to come into view, and there it was," Capote said. After reading the newspaper article, he abruptly decided to depart for Kansas "without any prejudices." One remarkable aspect of his subsequent investigations and research ("I wrote 6,000 pages of notes before I ever sat down to write the book") is that the completed product was to remain scrupulously free of editorializing. "The book wasn't something reconstructed from a great distance," he is quoted by Frankel as saying. "I did it right along as it was happening. I lived the whole thing." He continued, "I have a very detached attitude about work vis à vis myself. I think it's a very valuable quality to have if you want to do the work that I do. I feel detached, but that doesn't mean I don't feel moved." He expanded upon these sentiments in some remarks made to George Plimpton: "For the nonfiction novel to be entirely successful, the author should not appear in the work. Once the narrator does appear, he has to appear throughout, all the way down the line, and the I-I-I intrudes when it really shouldn't."[16]

In Cold Blood carries a dedication with it "For Jack Dunphy and Harper Lee with my love and gratitude." Dunphy is a fellow novelist and long-time friend, but it was Harper Lee who accompanied Truman Capote to Holcomb, Kansas. "I didn't exactly want to arrive out there all by myself, not knowing what I was walking into with the town in the grips of this immense murder case," he told Frankel. Miss Lee, acting in the role of "friend" and "assistant," obliged Capote with two months of research time, although the great bulk of the investigation was done by Capote personally. "I had to do so much more than research," Capote commented. "I used to have to write something up to ten letters a day to people just in connection with tiny little details."

Probably the most intriguing aspect of his reportorial under-taking was his relationship with the killers themselves. He told Frankel what gradually became self-evident, that "Hickock and Smith [became] very very good friends of mine . . . intimates in every conceivable way," although he initially encountered problems interviewing the men and gaining their confidence. According to one account,[17] Capote's first interview with Perry Smith revealed nothing; the killer "couldn't have been less communicative." Hickock, by contrast, "was someone you meet on a train, immensely garrulous, who starts up a conversation and is only too obliged to tell you *everything*." After the prisoners were committed to the Kansas State Penitentiary for Men, according to Professor Nance, "Capote secured permission to continue his interviews with them. These eventually numbered over two hundred. In addition, he began writing to each of them

twice a week and supplying them with books and magazines . . .
The prisoners were permitted to write twice a week and
faithfully did so."[18]

After Capote endured the grim ordeal of the prisoners'
execution, it was Capote, Professor Nance has written, who "paid
for the modest headstones that mark the graves of Perry and
Dick in a private cemetery near the prison."[19]

In Cold Blood was filmed under the direction of Richard
Brooks who, Capote said, was "the only director who agreed
with—and was willing to risk—my own concept of how the book
should be transferred to film."[20] Capote had two preconditions in
mind about the filming of the book that seemed to him of
greatest importance. The first of these was that the picture be
done in black and white, and the second, that the actors be "a
cast of unknowns—that is, actors without 'public faces.' "[21]
Because both author and director were concerned that the film
"duplicate reality," they resolved to film on location: "the house
of the murdered Clutter family; the same Kansas variety store
where Perry and Dick bought the rope and tape used to bind
their four victims; and certain courthouses, prisons, filling
stations, hotel rooms and highways and city streets—all those
places that they had seen in the course of their crime and its
aftermath."[22] Brooks made every possible effort to "duplicate
reality." Much of the Clutter furniture was still in the home.
Herbert Clutter's Stetson was perched on a hatrack. Nancy
Clutter's sheet music remained open at the piano, and her
brother Kenyon's glasses rested "on a bureau, the lens shimmer-
ing in sunlight." In their quest for fidelity to the crime itself,
Brooks was able to engage two actors (Robert Blake and Scott
Wilson) who bore an uncanny resemblance to the actual killers.
Capote found the similarity between the actors and the
murderers unnerving:

". . . it wasn't until I went to Kansas to follow the progress of the film
that I met them. And meeting them, having to be around them, was not
an experience I care to repeat. This has nothing to do with my reaction
to them as private individuals: they both are sensitive, seriously gifted
men. It's simply that despite the clear physical resemblance to the
original pair, their photographs had not prepared me for the
mesmerizing reality.
    Particularly Robert Blake. The first time I saw him I thought a ghost

had sauntered in out of the sunshine, slippery-haired and sleepy-eyed. I couldn't accept the idea that this was someone pretending to be Perry, he was Perry—and the sensation I felt was like a free fall down an elevator shaft . . . It was as though Perry had been resurrected but was suffering from amnesia and remembered me not at all."[23]

Critical reaction to *In Cold Blood* varied more than might have been expected. "The book has been executed without the finesse of which, at his best, [Capote] has been capable, and it is residually shallow," wrote Stanley Kauffmann in *The New Republic*.[24] F. W. Dupee's assessment was considerably higher: "*In Cold Blood* is the best documentary account of an American crime ever written," he said; ". . . for Mr. Capote the [Clutter case] is pristine material; and the book he has written about it is appropriately and impressively fresh."[25] William Phillips' review for *Commentary* contained a more mixed reaction: "Perhaps I can best sum up my response to the book by saying that when I finished it I thought it was good in its own way, but that the question remained—as in the old Jewish joke—whether *In Cold Blood* was good for literature . . . it is a good story, competently though too mechanically told, its smooth, standardized prose and somewhat contrived shifting of scenes giving off an aura of fictional skill and urbanity and imaginative recreation. *In Cold Blood* reads like high-class journalism, the kind of journalism one expects of a novelist."[26]

CHAPTER 5

The Anatomy of a Writer: Style, Characterization, Theme, and Influences

" **A**N ARTIST'S principal task," Capote said in his essay "A Voice from a Cloud" (1969), is "to tame and shape the raw creative vision."[1] His remark reflects, of course, the central task of all artists, which is to transform the largely unordered materials acquired through observation, into meaningful aesthetic form. Truman Capote's way of accomplishing this transformation, however, has not always been the same, inasmuch as his own "creative vision" has undergone some change over the years of his life in letters.

I Style

Capote has moved simultaneously over a period of time from being a fairly conventional writer of mediocre short stories (witness, for example, "The Walls are Cold," "A Mink of One's Own," and "The Shape of Things"), to both a lyric prose romancer and an objective reporter. In view of what has been said thus far, Capote's development in these two directions perhaps calls for some additional documentation. Suffice it to say that to read a few pages of *Other Voices, Other Rooms,* followed by such other retrospective and personal pieces as "Children on Their Birthdays," "Jug of Silver," *The Grass Harp, A Christmas Memory,* and *The Thanksgiving Visitor,* evidences Capote's considerable talent and predilection for the prose romance. But at the same time that these romantic impulses were finding creative outlet, he was also moving strongly in the direction of becoming a creative, but still objective reporter, as is most

119

evident in *Local Color, The Muses Are Heard*, "The Duke in His Domain," and finally, in *In Cold Blood*. This is not to suggest, however, that even at his most "objective," Capote had forsaken his gift as a romancer, or held it in abeyance, as both the first and the last paragraph of *In Cold Blood* will attest. In his initial paragraph, for example, he sketches the terrain in the midst of which Holcomb, Kansas, is situated:

". . . some seventy miles east of the Colorado border, the countryside, with its hard blue skies and desert-clear air, has an atmosphere that is rather more Far Western than Middle West. The local accent is barbed with a prairie twang, a ranch-hand nasalness, and the men, many of them, wear narrow frontier trousers, Stetsons, and high-heeled boots with pointed toes. The land is flat, and the views are awesomely extensive; horses, herds of cattle, a white cluster of grain elevators rising as gracefully as Greek temples are visible long before a traveler reaches them."

Prose of this texture is both imaginative and objective at the same time, illustrating in part the techniques of a fiction writer that Capote brought to the cause of his reporting.

It is generally known that the great mass of notes that formed the raw materials for *In Cold Blood* were sifted ruthlessly for what was usable in a factual and aesthetic sense, and that huge quantities of material were omitted. "Where there is no discipline, there is nothing," Capote once remarked.[2] The arrangement of selected detail, moreover, is one of the artist's more demanding problems. "Finding the right form for your story is simply to realize the most *natural* way of telling the story," he remarked on still another occasion. "The test of whether or not a writer has divined the natural shape of his story is just this: after reading it, can you imagine it differently, or does it silence your imagination and seem to be absolute and final?"[3] After Capote established himself as a mature and finished writer, his sense of form and his selectivity of detail have seldom failed him, except perhaps in a story called "The Headless Hawk," which is as loose and rambling as its protagonist, and in *The Grass Harp* at the point in the story where Sister Ida and her fifteen children enter the narrative. One of his overlooked triumphs is his single paragraph essay on Louis Armstrong which was printed in *Observations* (1959). Part of that paragraph reads,

. . . for me the sweet anger of Armstrong's trumpet, the froggy exuberance of his come-to-me-baby mouthings, are a piece of Proust's madeleine cake: they make Mississippi moons rise again, summon the muddy lights of river towns, the sound, like an alligator's yawn, of river horns—I hear the rush of the mulatto river pushing by, hear, always, stomp! stomp! the beat of the grinning Buddha's feet as he shouts his way into 'Sunny Side of the Street' and the honeymooning dancers, dazed with bootleg brew and sweating through their talcum, bunny-hug around the ship's saloony ballroom.

There can be little disagreement that Capote qualifies both as a southern regionalist and local colorist. He has denied being the former, but the evidence speaks louder than his denial: "I, personally, have never thought of myself as a writer regionally oriented. My first book [*Other Voices, Other Rooms*] had a southern setting because I was writing about what I knew most deeply at the time: the raw material of my work usually depends on events lived ten years beforehand (in fiction, not non-fiction). Now, of course, the South is so far behind me that it has ceased to furnish me with subject matter."[4]

Quite a number of Capote's pages, however, not only have the South as setting, but also convey a regionalist's response to his environment. Besides *Other Voices, Other Rooms*, southern settings prevail in almost half of what he has written, and among his own favorite contemporary American writers, moreover, are figures whose style and outlook are somewhat similar to his own, notably Flannery O'Connor, Eudora Welty, and Katherine Anne Porter. And yet not all of Capote's local color writing is devoted to the South, as his pieces on Haiti, Brooklyn, and Ischia demonstrate. But to see Capote as a southern local colorist is to recognize his penchant for a kind of gothic horror that in part characterized southern writers from Poe to Faulkner. In *Other Voices, Other Rooms* is, for example, a description of "a tall queer tottering ginger-colored house" which is described in the American gothic tradition: "the windows of the house are cracked and shattered, hollow as eyeless sockets; a rotted balcony leans perilously forward, and yellow sunflower birds hide their nests in secret places; the scaling outer walls are ragged with torn, weather-faded posters that flutter when there is a wind. Among the town kids it is a sign of great valor to enter these black rooms after dark and signal with a match flame from a window on the topmost floor."

The gothic mode is present, if far less emphasized, in *The Grass Harp,* where the protagonist, Colin Fenwick, is preoccupied by death and burial, and in a number of the short stories ("Miriam," "The Headless Hawk," and particularly "A Tree of Night") traces of the gothic mode are present, even though the first two of these stories are set outside the South. *In Cold Blood,* obviously, contains much of this gothic horror, particularly in the description of Bobby Rupp's visit to the Phillips' Funeral Home where he finds the four coffins of the murdered Clutter family, and the head of each victim encased in a huge ball of cotton to conceal the mutilations of shotgun blasts.

No reader at all acquainted with Capote's body of writing can fail to notice his preference for satiric comedy, the bulk of which is directed at two objects: provincial life and provincial tastes. His treatments of the former (some of which are dealt with sympathetically in *A Christmas Memory*) are handled with a touch of levity, as in *Other Voices, Other Rooms* where, for example, in Noon City "the men sport their finest shirts and store-bought breeches" and where "the women scent themselves with vanilla flavoring or dime-store perfume, of which the most popular brand is called La Divine." There is hardly more of Capote's satire of small-town life than in the pages of *The Grass Harp* where con-man Morris Ritz lives "in the best room at the Lola Hotel and [eats] steak dinners at Phil's Café." "Children on Their Birthdays," which is partly a satire on small-town living, contains the character Manny Fox who, like Morris Ritz, is the city slicker who gulls most of the provincials with improbable ruses, and then skips town.

Capote's comic treatment of persons with questionable taste occurs with considerable frequency. Miss Wisteria, for example, appears in a dress "of purple silk tied about the middle with a yellow silk sash" in *Other Voices, Other Rooms.* A little girl in *The Grass Harp* bears the name Texaco Gasoline "because those were such pretty words." In "The Muses Are Heard," as has been mentioned, Capote draws attention to the Russian peasant who finds it amusing to force beer through his hollow eye socket while affecting a parody of Christ on the Cross. The story "A Tree of Night" has in it a woman who, when the need arises, blows her nose in her petticoat hem.

Much of Capote's work is marked by a kind of concealed documentation. F. W. Dupee's comment about *In Cold Blood* is to the point: "the documentation is, for the most part, suppressed in the text—presumably in order to supply the narrative with a surface of persuasive immediacy and impenetrable omniscience."[5] All three of Capote's longer fictional works, *Other Voices, Other Rooms, The Grass Harp,* and *Breakfast at Tiffany's,* are veiled, loosely autobiographic tales that reflect to some limited extent the author's personal history. The sketches in *Local Color* also contain this veiled documentation of the author's having lived in the places about which he writes: New Orleans, New York, Brooklyn, and other similarly colorful locations. *The Muses Are Heard,* "The Duke in His Domain," and *In Cold Blood*—all three of which were written for *The New Yorker*—are pieces in which "facts" are handled at the same time both literally and impressionistically.

A large portion of Capote's writing is invested with a sense of mystery, ranging from simple intrigue to all-pervasive gothic horror. The reader can scarcely forget the "luminous green legs that shine under the dark marsh water like drowned corpses" in *Other Voices, Other Rooms.* Certain of the short stories contain a measure of mystery and wonderment, especially "A Tree of Night," "Miriam," and "Shut a Final Door." But *In Cold Blood* puts mystery and horror to work for something more than effect when the reader is taken into the minds of two murderers to explore, among other things, questions of motivation and criminal intent.

Part of Capote's literary style is characterized by the recurrence of motifs, for the purpose of achieving unity of tone and effect. One of these images is that of guitars. It is in *Other Voices, Other Rooms,* for example, that Randolph speaks of having met Dolores in Spain: "she had over thirty guitars, and played all of them, I must admit, quite horridly." In *The Grass Harp* Capote pictures Little Homer "sprawled with his back against a tombstone [picking] melancholy notes on a guitar." One of the items that Holly Golightly leaves behind when she departs for Brazil in *Breakfast at Tiffany's* is a guitar, just as two other fictional characters (Kay in "A Tree of Night" and Tico Feo in "A Diamond Guitar") are closely identified with guitars. Even Perry Smith, one of the two killers in *In Cold Blood,* is seen at one point in the book "clutching the old Gibson guitar, his most beloved possession," which is later stolen from him in Acapulco.

Another recurrent image in Capote's work is food, an image used either to achieve a better sense of local color or to seize upon an apt subject for sensuous description. It is in *Other Voices, Other Rooms* that Joel Knox, newly arrived in Skully's Landing, sits before a breakfast of "fried eggs and grits, sopping with sausage gravy." And in "Greek Paragraphs" (from *Local Color*) Capote writes of devouring "peaches the size of cantaloupes and the color of cantaloupe meat. Peaches of a deliciously yielding texture and a juicy liquor-like sweetness." Holly Golightly prepares notorious dishes in *Breakfast at Tiffany's* that are as unusual as her own bizarre character: "Nero-ish novelties (roasted pheasant stuffed with pomegranates and persimmons) and other dubious innovations (chicken and saffron rice served with chocolate sauce: 'an East Indian classic, *my* dear')." She also prepares something called "Tobacco Tapioca," which the narrator prudently decides he had "best not describe."

Other recurrent images, such as knives, appear with a certain frequency throughout Capote's work: for example in *Other Voices, Other Rooms* in which much is made of Keg's having cut Zoo's throat and Joel Knox is given Papadaddy's (Jesus Fever's) "fine handsome sword." Tico Feo and Goober, who appear in "A Diamond Guitar," are both committed to the prison farm as a result of knifing incidents, and Olivia-Ann in "My Side of the Matter" is shown "whittling on a stick with her fourteen-inch hog knife." Knives also play a part that may have attracted Capote to the Clutter murders, for Perry Smith in *In Cold Blood* matter-of-factly confesses to having cut Herbert Clutter's throat prior to shooting him in the head.

A more pleasant, and perhaps more important, image to be found occasionally is that of trees and the security they represent in Capote's fiction. In Joel Knox's moment of self-realization in *Other Voices,* it may be recalled, he "looked about for a tree to climb: he would go right to the very top." Here he finds both solace and a sense of freedom. In *The Grass Harp,* however, the significance of a house built atop two China trees becomes most clear: "their branches were so embraced that you could step from one into the other; in fact, they were bridged by a tree-house: spacious, sturdy, a model of a tree-house . . ." It is to this house built in two trees that several characters both retreat from society at the same time that they search for self-awareness. It is as if they are temporarily lifted (metaphorically and literally) above the mundane and workaday concerns of the rest of the population for this relatively short period of time. The reader may notice that essentially the same idea occurs in the short story "A Diamond Guitar"; the escape plan of the prison farm inmates calls first for a run through a creek to avoid leaving a scent for bloodhounds to pick up and then hiding out in a tree until darkness descends. For Tico Feo, the plan works, and he makes good his escape.

A thorough reading of Capote will reveal also that much of his work is predicated upon travel. Both *Local Color* and *The Muses Are Heard* are indebted to the travel book genre. Elsewhere, however, his writing often involves extensive travel; for example, the elaborate flight to avoid capture that Perry Smith and Richard Hickock embark upon after the Clutter murders, not to mention the gypsy lives the two killers lived before the crime transpired. In *Other Voices, Other Rooms* the protagonist Joel Knox began a search for a father and for a sense of identity that carried him throughout the South. Holly Golightly of *Breakfast at Tiffany's* is also an inveterate traveller in search of essentially the same things that Joel Knox is seeking: self-understanding and a place in the world. It is Holly's memorable Tiffany calling card, after all, that reads: *Miss Holiday Golightly, Traveling.* A few of the short stories use the travel motif fairly extensively, among them "The Shape of Things," which has as its setting a moving train, as does most of "A Tree of Night." The child protagonists of "Miriam," "Jug of Silver," and "Children on Their Birthdays" are all vagabonds of one sort or another, as are Sister Ida and her fifteen progeny in *The Grass Harp.*

There are occasions when Capote, like his predecessors Poe and Dostoevsky, makes use of the *doppelgänger,* or double-image. One appears at the beginning of the ninth chapter of *Other Voices Other Rooms* when little Sunshine covers the mirror in Jesus Fever's room so that in the event of Jesus Fever's death, his soul will not be trapped in the mirror. Doubles appear in at least two of the short stories—in "Miriam" where, as has been explained, the child and the middle-aged woman appear to be, in reality, facets of the same personality, and in the gruesome short story "Shut a Final Door" where the phantom telephone caller who plagues Walter Ranney is apparently a part of Ranney himself. Capote used the idea of the double again in *In Cold Blood* when he notes that Perry Smith is given to mirror-gazing, a practice that his partner in crime Dick Hickock finds annoying: "Everytime you see a mirror you go into a trance, like. Like you was looking at some georgeous piece of butt."

Death is an omnipresent reality in a great deal of Capote's work. There is a succession of deaths in *Other Voices, Other Rooms* beginning with Joel Knox's parents, and *In Cold Blood* not only the four members of the Clutter family die, but also their killers, in addition to certain others who die from natural causes. Death also plays a prominent role in the short stories where, for example, in "A Tree of Night" the two con-artists have as their game the fraudulent simulation of death and burial. In "Preacher's Legend" and later in "Among the Paths to Eden" are protagonists who are especially mindful of the passing of their wives. "Children on Their Birthdays" ends with the death of Lily Jane Bobbit, and *A Christmas Memory* amounts partly to a wistful, backward glance at Capote's believed Sook Faulk.

Much of what Capote has written places emphasis upon dreams (experienced both in sleep and in wakefulness) that his characters have. In the 1947 story "Shut a Final Door" the protagonist Walter Ranney "dreamed of an old castle where only old turkeys lived, and dreamed a dream involving his father. . . ." "Master Misery," which was published two years later, is expressly concerned with the necessity of maintaining dreams, and in this story the characters, it may be recalled, market their dreams to the mysterious Mr. Revercomb. When *Other Voices, Other Rooms* appeared, Capote made much of the significance of dreaming, for here the character Randolph tells Joel Knox that he has discovered Dolores' dream book: "Every morning Dolores wrote out her night's dreams in a big scrapbook she kept concealed under a mattress; she wrote them sometimes in French, more often in German or English, but whatever the language, the content was always malevolent." When *In Cold Blood* appeared, it too placed some importance on of the dreams of certain of its characters. Dick Hickock, for example, regards Perry Smith, a person with an unusually active fantasy life, as "too much 'the dreamer,' " whereas Hickock says of himself, "I'm a normal. I only dream about blond chicken." Smith, however, comes by his tendency to daydream honestly, for it was his father Tex who "taught his son to dream of gold." After the murders have been committed, the murdered Bonnie Clutter appears to Alvin Dewey's wife Marie in a dream. Says Marie: "I was cooking supper, and suddenly Bonnie walked through the door. She was wearing a blue angora sweater, and she looked so sweet and pretty, and I said, 'Oh Bonnie . . . Bonnie, dear . . . I haven't seen you since that terrible thing happened." But she didn't answer, only looked at me in that shy way of hers, and I didn't know how to go on."

Probably the only other prevalent recurring motif in Capote's writing is that of family disunity and discord, a motif that is obviously and understandably autobiographic in origin. Family disunity is, after all, the thing that sets *Other Voices, Other Rooms* into motion, since its protagonist Joel Knox has been bandied from place to place to live after the death of his mother. In *The Grass Harp*, however, Colin Fenwick is living with his two distant relatives because of the deaths of both of his parents. And when Joel Knox and Colin Fenwick are re-situated with surrogate parents, the discord, as has been made clear, continues. The notion of family disunity continues in *Breakfast at Tiffany's* in which Holly Golightly has left her husband and children back in Texas to live a more adventuresome life in New York.

Among the short stories, the comic "My Side of the Matter" is concerned with marital and family difficulties besetting the narrator that are no laughing matter: "I know what is being said about me and you can take my side or theirs, that's your own business," says he. In "Jug of Silver" the bedraggled child protagonist Appleseed, along with his siblings, is part of a nomadic family that traverses the South, barely one step ahead of the law. At the concusion of *A Christmas Memory* the narrator Buddy is finally cut apart from all family ties: "Home is where my friend is, and there I never go." But in *The Thanksgiving Visitor* Capote was closer still to the autobiography and the specific circumstances of his own gypsy-like childhood, saying as he does that his own family having been broken, he was taken in by "distant relatives, elderly cousins . . . three maiden ladies and their bachelor brother. . . ."

Finally, Capote was to make much of the history of family discord and disunity that produced the two killers Perry Smith and Richard Hickock of *In Cold Blood*. Hickock himself has been "twice married, twice divorced, now twenty-eight and the father of three boys" and has been granted "parole on the condition that he reside with his parents." His accomplice Smith has also come from unfortunate circumstances. Smith recalls that once "my mother was 'entertaining' some sailors while my father was away. When he came home a fight ensued, and my father, after a violent struggle, threw the sailors out & proceeded to beat my mother. I was frightfully scared, in fact all us children were terrified."

II Characterization

There are certain character "types" that recur in Capote's writing, some of which (the eccentric, the grotesque, the fraud, the "Wizard Man") have been mentioned in earlier discussions. Two character groupings occur especially frequently in Capote's work. The first of these is the child-as-seeker (an autobiographic portrait) of which there are four obvious examples: Joel Knox in *Other Voices, Other Rooms*, Colin Fenwick in *The Grass Harp*, Buddy in *A Christmas Memory*, and Buddy again in *The Thanksgiving Visitor*. By whatever name he goes by, the child is searching for identity, a home, a parent, and a sense of direction in the world about him.

The second of these character types is the victim, a character with many faces and identities. One such character is the bedridden and helpless Ed Sansom of *Other Voices, Other Rooms* who has been all but mortally wounded by Randolph. Another is Dolly Talbo of *The Grass Harp*, whose dropsy cure causes her to be the envy and the victim of her overly enterprising sister Verena. While it may be unnecessary to point out that Capote's most victimized victims are the four members of the ill-fated Clutter family in *In Cold Blood*, Capote demonstrates that their victimizers are also products of their own unhappy past.

The victim, however, has a fairly long history which reaches back into Capote's short stories, beginning with "The Walls Are Cold," where an essentially innocent young sailor is tricked as part of a sexual ploy conceived in the mind of a fickle teen-aged girl. In his next story, "A Mink of One's Own," a woman is duped into paying four hundred dollars for what turns out to be a worthless mink coat. "The Shape of Things" involves a young service man whose mental faculties have been severely impaired as a result of his wartime experiences. An essentially witty story,

"My Side of the Matter" depicts a callow young man whose ill-advised marriage has been further jeopardized by his young wife's interfering relatives, and whose prospects of weathering the marriage are exceedingly remote. The story "Miriam," as has been noted, is essentially a tale of victimization wherein a middle-aged woman comes under the power of a young girl who is her alter ego. The story that followed this, "A Tree of Night," is yet another tale having primarily to do with systematic victimization, and in "Shut a Final Door" the protagonist Walter Ranney is defeated, like the woman in "Miriam," by forces within himself that he is unable to control. Similarly, in "Master Misery" Sylvia and Oreilly are both defeated characters, she by a certain inability to cope with the world, he by alcohol. It is Sylvia, in turn, who resembles the mentally crippled D. J. in "The Headless Hawk." One of the more pathetic and heart-rending victims is Miss Lily Jane Bobbit, the child protagonist in "Children on Their Birthdays," who is run down by a bus at the end of the story.

Another character "type" that demands comment is that of the free-spiritied vagabond, a character who is refreshingly free and enviably unfettered in the world. There are at least three prominent examples of this decidedly nonvictimized character; one is the prostitute Ottilie who appears in "House of Flowers"; another is the airy Tico Feo ("A Diamond Guitar") who strums plaintively on his glass-studded guitar and who succeeds in escaping from the confines of a prison farm. But the best example of all is Holly Golightly whose life in *Breakfast at Tiffany's* is almost ideally tailored to her own whim, and who, like Ottilie and Tico Feo, lives in a world that is outside the reach of the law. All three, however, are distinctly exotic characters whose lives contrast vividly with those of the more numerous victims in Capote's work.

III *Theme*

Whereas it is sometimes possible to view the writing of other authors as a unified whole, the numerous and varied products of Capote's literary career tend to resist categorization and thematic generalization. However, certain thematic patterns can be identified, if not universally applied to everything he has written in the past thirty years. Some of these patterns have been cited in previous pages, and they lead to the general conclusion that Capote writes most often retrospectively, with attention to childhood and adolescent adventures that relate to problems of initiation, of coming of age, of growing up in a world beset with danger and insecurity. Certainly, these generalizations apply to his longer and more acclaimed pieces such as *Other Voices, Other Rooms, The Grass Harp, Breakfast at Tiffany's, A Christmas Memory, The Thanksgiving Visitor,* and even *In Cold Blood;* for in each of these is the problem of childhood or adolescent mentality in its uncertain struggle to somehow "adjust" to the demands of approaching adult "responsibility." To fail in this crucial adjustment is to be victimized or to victimize others. To succeed in the adjustment process is to live a life that is relatively satisfying because it is free, unrestricted, and directed from within.

At the risk of repetition, perhaps a few examples of this archetypal challenge to find accommodation in the world may suffice. The reader has the distinct impression that one group of Capote characters seem to succeed at handling the stresses of life, while another group does not. Characters such as Joel Knox, Colin Fenwick, Holly Golightly, Buddy, Appleseed, Lily Jane Bobbit, Tico Feo, and Ottilie have somehow come to terms with the world, for the general reason that they have somewhere along the line come to terms with themselves by learning who they are; they rely successfully on inner resources. They either do learn or have learned to manage themselves through what may best be called self-reliance.

Another set of Capote characters have not acquired this crucial independence, nor have they any prospects of finding it, because the passing of childhood means that they have also passed the opportunity to learn who they are, and it is now too late to find out. Consequently, they are ones who, because of the failure to resolve this perplexing riddle of identity, make themselves, and others, generally miserable. Seven examples of this kind of character, among the many to be found in Capote's writing, may suffice: Kay, Sylvia, Walter Ranney, Miriam (the elder), D. J., and the two most infamous characters, the killers Perry Smith and Richard Hickock, whose unfortunate start in the world was largely responsible for what was to become of them.

IV *Influences*

I,ike most writers, Truman Capote is an avid and interested reader. The extent to which he has been influenced by other writers is partly conjectural, although his own remarks about his preferences in other writers may provide some insights about his own achievement as writer. In 1972 he wrote, "Really, I like to read. I always have. There are not many contemporary writers I like too well. Though I have admired, among our own Americans, the late Flannery O'Connor, and Norman Mailer, William Styron, Eudora Welty, Katherine Anne Porter, the early [J. D.] Salinger . . . But for the last decade or so I prefer to read writers I've already read. Proven wine. Proust. Flaubert. Jane Austen. Raymond Chandler (one of the *great* American artists). Dickens (I had read all of Dickens before I was sixteen, and have just now completed the full cycle again)."[6] The most exhaustive study of the relationships and influences of other writers with Capote has been documented by Melvin J Friedman, who discusses such writers as William Faulkner, Carson McCullers, Flannery O'Connor, as well as Alain Robbe-Grillet, and an array of other non-American writers.[7]

Relationships and influences aside, however, that Capote has created a world and a sensibility all his own is a reality not to be lost track of. In this regard, perhaps Paul Levine best summed up the matter of Capote's achievement when he commented that "While we must acknowledge Capote's admission that 'style is the mirror of an artist's sensibility—more so than the *content* of his work,' we must also recognize that there is no dearth of content in his work. To understand that content fully we must first posit some very elemental points, because Capote is to a great extent an erudite writer about primal things. At the heart of his writing is the dichotomy in the world between good and evil, the daylight and the nocturnal, man and nature, and between the internal and external manifestations of things."[8]

Notes and References

Chapter One

1. "Checking in With Truman Capote," *Esquire*, Nov. 1972, p. 136.
2. Ibid., p. 187.
3. "Silhouettes and Souvenirs," *New York Times Book Review*, Oct. 28, 1973, p. 35.
4. *The Dogs Bark* (New York, 1973), pp. 405, 406.
5. Ibid., p. 409.
6. Ibid., p. 410.
7. *The Americans* (New York, 1970), p. 19.
8. Ibid., p. 24.
9. *Esquire*, Dec., 1970, p. 258.
10. Cynthia Ozick, "Reconsideration," *New Republic*, Jan. 27, 1973, p. 31.
11. Roy Newquist, *Counterpoint*, (Chicago, 1964), p. 76.
12. *The Dogs Bark*, p. 5. Craig M. Goad in *Dictionary of Literary Biography* (Detroit, 1978), II, 81, identifies these schools as Trinity and St. John's Academy in New York, and the Greenwich, Connecticut, public schools.
13. *The Dogs Bark*, p. 414.
14. Ibid.
15. Ibid., pp. 417–418.
16. Ibid., p. 419.
17. Malcolm Cowley (ed.), *Writers at Work: The Paris Review Interviews*, (New York, 1960), p. 288.
18. Ibid.
19. Ibid.
20. Rochelle Girson, "48's Nine," *Saturday Review of Literature*, Feb. 12, 1949, p. 13.
21. Gloria Steinem, "Go Right Ahead and Ask Me Anything," *McCalls*, Nov. 1967, p. 151.
22. *The Americans*, p. 18.
23. Cowley, p. 289.
24. Steinem, p. 150.
25. Gerald Clarke, p. 188.
26. Cowley, p. 289.
27. William L. Nance, *The Worlds of Truman Capote*, (New York, 1970), p. 13.

28. Stanley Kunitz (ed.), Twentieth Century Authors, (New York, 1955), p. 167.
29. See Frost, p. 18. Also Steinem, p. 151.
30. *The Dogs Bark*, p. 5.
31. Ibid.
32. Girson, p. 13.
33. Kunitz, p. 168.
34. Steinem, p. 151.
35. Clarke, p. 188.
36. Ibid.
37. *The Dogs Bark*, p. 413.
38. Ibid.
39. Kunitz, p. 168.
40. *The Dogs Bark*, p. 8.
41. Nance, p. 14.
42. Ozick, p. 31.
43. Newquist, pp. 77, 78.
44. Harvey Breit, "A Talk with Truman Capote," *New York Times Book Review*, Feb. 24, 1952, p. 29.
45. Michael Kernan, "Capote Covers Texas Murder Trial," *Cincinnati Enquirer*, Jan. 10, 1974, p. 34.
46. Ibid.
47. Ibid.
48. Steinem, p. 150.
49. Ibid.
50. *Selected Writings*, (New York, 1963), p. 277.
51. Newquist, p. 79.
52. *The Dogs Bark*, p. 414.
53. Newquist, p. 79.
54. Ibid., p. 82.
55. *The Dogs Bark*, p. 10.
56. Ibid., pp. 10-11.
57. *The Dogs Bark*, p. 415.
58. Ibid.
59. Ibid., pp. 409-410.
60. Ibid., p. 409.
61. Granville Hicks, "Literary Horizons—The Story of an American Tragedy," *Saturday Review*, Jan. 22, 1966, p. 37.
62. Anon., "Come With Mr. Capote to a Masked Ball," *Life*, Dec. 9, 1966, p. 107.
63. Jane Howard, "A Host With a Genius for Jarring Juxtapositions," *Life*, Dec. 9, 1966, p. 117.
64. Anon., *Time*, Dec. 9, 1966, p. 88.
65. Anon. *The New York Times*, Oct. 23, 1970, p. 37.
66. Steinem, p. 149.

67. Clarke, p. 187.
68. Ibid.
69. Kernan, p. 34.
70. Capote, "Truman Capote on Christmas, Places, Memories," *Mademoiselle*, Dec. 1971, p. 123.

Chapter Two

1. Malcolm Cowley (ed.), *Writers at Work: The Paris Review Interviews*, (New York, 1960), p. 287.
2. Ibid., p. 290.
3. Ibid.
4. Roy Newquist, *Conterpoint* (Chicago, 1964), p. 80.

Chapter Three

1. *Radical Innocence: Studies in the Contemporary American Novel* (Princeton, N.J., 1961), p. 244.
2. *The Worlds of Truman Capote* (New York, 1970), p. 63.
3. "Two American Writers," *Sewanee Review*, Summer, 1960, p. 478.
4. Roy Newquist, *Counterpoint* (Chicago, 1964), p. 80.
5. *The Worlds of Truman Capote*, p. 62.
6. Malcolm Cowley, (ed.) *Writers at Work: The Paris Review Interviews*, (New York, 1960), p. 290.
7. *A Handbook to Literature*, Third Edition, (New York and Indianapolis, 1972), p. 459.
8. "Truman Capote Matures and Mellows," *New York Herald Tribune Book Review*, Sept. 30, 1951, p. 4.
9. "Sunlit Gothic," *Saturday Review of Literature*, Oct. 20, 1951, p. 19.
10. *Georgia Review*, Fall, 1959, p. 350.

Chapter Four

1. Roy Newquist, *Counterpoint* (Chicago, 1964), p. 78.
2. Ibid., p. 83.
3. Malcolm Cowley (ed.) *Writers at Work: The Paris Review Interviews* (New York, 1960), p. 291.
4. Granville Hicks, *Saturday Review*, Jan. 22, 1966, p. 35.
5. H. Frankel, "Author," *Saturday Review*, Jan. 22, 1966, p. 37.
6. Cowley, p. 291.
7. George Plimpton, "The Story Behind a Noncfiction Novel," *New York Times Book Review*, Jan. 16, 1966, p. 2.
8. Newquist.

9. Plimpton, p. 3.
10. Ibid.
11. Shana Alexander, "A Nonfictional Visit With Truman Capote," *Life,* Feb. 18, 1966, p. 22.
12. Ibid.
13. William L. Nance, *The Worlds of Truman Capote* (New York, 1970), p. 210.
14. L. Nichols, "Mr. Capote," *New York Times Book Review,* Aug. 22, 1965, p. 43.
15. Ibid., p. 39.
16. Plimpton, p. 38.
17. Ibid., p. 32.
18. Nance, p. 174.
19. Ibid., p. 176.
20. *The Dogs Bark* (New York, 1973), p. 398.
21. Ibid.
22. Ibid.
23. Ibid., p. 396.
24. *The New Republic,* Jan. 22, 1966, p. 19.
25. *The New York Review of Books,* Feb. 3, 1966, p. 3.
26. *Commentary,* May, 1966, p. 77.

Chapter Five

1. *The Dogs Bark,* (New York, 1973), p. 7.
2. Roy Newquist, *Counterpoint,* (Chicago, 1964), p. 81.
3. Malcolm Cowley (ed.), *Writers at Work: The Paris Review Interviews,* (New York, 1960), p. 287.
4. Newquist, p. 4.
5. "Truman Capote's Score," *New York Review of Books,* Feb. 3, 1966, p. 3.
6. *The Dogs Bark,* pp. 405, 406.
7. "Towards an Aesthetic: Truman Capote's Other Voices," in Irving Malin (ed.), *Truman Capote's In Cold Blood: A Critical Handbook* (Belmont, California, 1968), pp. 163–176.
8. "Truman Capote: The Revelation of the Broken Image," *Virginia Quarterly Review,* 34 (Autumn, 1958), 601.

Selected Bibliography

PRIMARY SOURCES

This bibliography is based on Robert J. Stanton's *Truman Capote: A Reference Guide* (Boston: G. K. Hall, 1980). For further details about reprints and foreign editions, consult the Stanton Guide. Detailed information about publications and reprints through 1967 is also contained in Jackson R. Bryer's "Truman Capote: A Bibliography," which is included in Irving Malin's *Truman Capote's "In Cold Blood": A Critical Handbook* (Belmont, Cal.: Wadsworth, 1969), pp. 239–69.

1. *Novels and Short Story Collections*

Breakfast at Tiffany's: A Short Novel and Three Stories. New York: Random House, 1958. [Contains "A Diamond Guitar," "The House of Flowers," and "A Christmas Memory."]
A Christmas Memory. New York: Random House, 1966.
The Grass Harp. New York: Random House, 1951.
Other Voices, Other Rooms. New York: Random House, 1948.
The Thanksgiving Visitor. New York: Random House, 1968.
A Tree of Night and Other Stories. New York: Random House, 1949. [Contains, besides the title story, "Children on Their Birthdays," "The Headless Hawk," "Master Misery," "Miriam," "My Side of the Matter," "Shut a Final Door."]

2. *Plays and Film Scripts*

Beat the Devil (Romulus Films, 1953). London: Romulus-Santana Productions, 1953.
The Grass Harp: A Play. New York: Random House, 1952. [Complete text appears also in *Theatre Arts,* September 1952, pp. 34–64.]
House of Flowers (a playscript by Capote, with lyrics by Capote and Harold Arlen, and music by Arlen). New York: Random House, 1968.
Trilogy: An Experiment in Multimedia (by Capote, with Frank and Eleanor Perry; introduction by John M. Culkin). New York: Macmillan, 1969. [Contains Capote's stories "Miriam," "Among the

Paths to Eden," and "A Christmas Memory," and the scripts based on them for the Perrys' film *Trilogy*.]

3. *Nonfiction*

The Dogs Bark: Public People and Private Places. New York: Random House, 1973.
In Cold Blood: A True Account of a Multiple Murder and Its Consequences. New York: Random House, 1965.
Local Color. New York: Random House, 1950. [Contains "New Orleans," "New York," "Brooklyn," "Hollywood," "Haiti," "To Europe," "Ischia," "Tangier," "A Ride through Spain."]
The Muses Are Heard. New York: Random House, 1956.
Observations: Photographs by Richard Avedon; Comments by Truman Capote. New York: Simon and Schuster, 1959.

4. *Collections of Writings*

The Grass Harp and A Tree of Night and Other Stories. New York: New American Library (paper), 1956.
Selected Writings of Truman Capote. New York: Random House, 1963. [Contains all the stories from *A Tree of Night* and *Breakfast at Tiffany's*, along with *The Muses are Heard;* "New Orleans," "Ischia," and "A Ride through Spain" from *Local Color;* "Among the Paths to Eden," "The Duke in His Domain," and "A House on the Heights."]

5. *Short Stories* (original periodical publications arranged chronologically).

"The Walls Are Cold," *Decade of Short Stories*, 4 (Fourth Quarter, 1943), 27-30.
"A Mink of One's Own," *Decade of Short Stories*, 6 (Third Quarter, 1944), 1-4.
"The Shape of Things," *Decade of Short Stories*, 6 (Fourth Quarter, 1944), 21-23.
[All three of the above are uncollected.]
"My Side of the Matter," *Story*, 26 (May-June, 1945), 34-40.
"Miriam," *Mademoiselle*, June, 1945, 114-15, 184, 186-90.
"A Tree of Night," *Harper's Bazaar*, October, 1945, pp. 110, 176-88.
"Jug of Silver," *Mademoiselle*, December, 1945, pp. 142-43, 238-47.
"Preacher's Legend," *Prairie Schooner*, 19 (December, 1945), 265-74 [uncollected].
"The Headless Hawk," *Harper's Bazaar*, November, 1946, pp. 254-55, 330-58.

"Shut a Final Door," *Atlantic Monthly*, August, 1947, pp. 49-55.
"Children on Their Birthdays," *Mademoiselle*, January, 1949, pp. 88-90, 146-51.
"Master Misery," *Horizon*, 19 (January, 1949), 19-37; *Harper's Magazine*, February, 1949, pp. 38-48.
"A Diamond Guitar," *Harper's Bazaar*, November, 1950, pp. 164, 170-78, 188.
"House of Flowers," *Botthege Oscure*, 6 (1950), 414-29.
"A Christmas Memory," *Mademoiselle*, December, 1956, pp. 70-71, 125-31.
"Breakfast at Tiffany's," *Esquire*, November, 1958, pp. 134-62.
"Among the Paths to Eden," *Esquire*, July, 1960, pp. 53-57.
"The Thanksgiving Visitor," *McCalls*, November, 1967, pp. 75, 155-62.

6. *Essays* (original periodical publications arranged chronologically).

"Notes on N.O.," *Harper's Bazaar*, October, 1946, pp. 268-71, 361-62.
"Brooklyn Notes," *Junior Bazaar*, September, 1947, pp. 104-05, 125-28.
"This Winter's Mask," *Harper's Bazaar*, December, 1947, pp. 100-05, 195-96. [Uncollected review of ten current Broadway plays.]
"Call It New York," *Vogue*, February 1, 1948, pp. 193, 258-59.
"Haitian Notes," *Harper's Bazaar*, December, 1948, pp. 120, 165-73.
"Faulkner Dances," *Theatre Arts*, April, 1949, p. 49. [Uncollected review]
"The Bridge of Childhood," *Mademoiselle*, May, 1949, pp. 91, 144-61. [Autobiographical]
"Tangier," *Vogue*, April 1, 1950, pp. 120-21, 166-67.
"Isola d'Ischia," *Mademoiselle*, May, 1950, pp. 110-11, 166-68.
"A Ride through Spain," *New Yorker*, September 2, 1950, pp. 42-45.
"A House in Sicily," *Harper's Bazaar*, January, 1951, pp. 116-17, 153-55.
"La Divine," *Harper's Bazaar*, April, 1952, pp. 148-49. [Uncollected praise of Greta Garbo]
"Onward and Upward with the Arts—Porgy and Bess in Russia," *New Yorker*, October 20, 1956, pp. 38-105; October 27, 1956, pp. 41-114. [Published as *The Muses are Heard.*]
"Profiles—The Duke in His Domain," *New Yorker*, November 9, 1957, pp. 53-100. [About Marlon Brando]
"Brooklyn Heights: A Personal Memoir," *Holiday*, February, 1959, pp. 64-68, 112-15.
"Maya Plisetskaya," *Harper's Bazaar*, September 1959, pp. 182-83.
"Observations on Ezra Pound," *Esquire*, September, 1959, pp. 74-76.
"A Gathering of Swans," *Harper's Bazaar*, October, 1959, pp. 122-25.
"New Focus on Familiar Faces," *Life*, October 12, 1959, pp. 136-45.

[The four pieces above comment on photographs by Richard Avedon and are collected in *Observations*.]

"The $6 Misunderstanding," *New York Review of Books*, May 1963, pp. 14-15. [Uncollected unfavorable review of Michel Butor's novel *Mobile*.]

"Plisetskaya: 'A Two-Headed Calf,' " *Vogue*, April 1, 1964, pp. 168-71.

"A Curious Gift," *Redbook*, June, 1965, pp. 52, 92-94. [Autobiographical]

"Annals of Crime—In Cold Blood," *New Yorker*, September 25, 1965, pp. 57-166; October 2, 1965, pp. 57-175; October 9, 1965, pp. 58-183; October 16, 1965, pp. 62-193. [Published as *In Cold Blood*, 1965.]

"The 'Sylvia' Odyssey," *Vogue*, January 15, 1966, pp. 68-75.

"Two Faces and . . . a Landscape," *Vogue*, February 1, 1966, pp. 144-49. [A discussion of Capote's relationship with Perry Smith and Richard Hickock.]

"The Guts of a Butterfly," London *Observer*, March 27, 1966, p. 21. [Angry reply to Kenneth Tynan's review of *In Cold Blood*.]

"Oliver Smith," *McCalls*, October, 1966, pp. 102-03.

"Truman Capote Introduces Jane Bowles," *Mademoiselle*, December, 1966, 114-16. [Also appears as an Introduction to *The Collected Works of Jane Bowles*, New York: Farrar, Straus & Giroux, 1966.]

"Truman Capote . . . and Many, Many More Remember the Books from Childhood They Loved Best," *Ladies' Home Journal*, December, 1966, pp. 20, 24, 29.

" 'Extreme Magic': An Awake-Dream, Cruising up the Yugoslavian Coast," *Vogue*, April 15, 1967, pp. 84-89, 146-47.

"Voice from a Cloud," *Harper's Magazine*, November, 1967, pp. 99-100. [Recollections reprinted as a preface to the twentieth-anniversary edition of *Other Voices, Other Rooms*.]

"Truman Capote Reports on the Filming of 'In Cold Blood,' " *Saturday Evening Post*, January 13, 1968, pp. 62-65.

"Death Row, U.S.A.," *Esquire*, October, 1968, pp. 194-99.

"Time, the Timeless, and Beaton's Time Sequences," *Vogue*, November 1, 1968, pp. 172, 232-33. [Reprinted as "Introduction" to *The Best of Beaton*, New York: Macmillan, 1968.]

"At the Sea and in the City," *House Beautiful*, April, 1969, pp. 93-98.

"Donna Marcella and the Avocato," *Vogue*, April 1, 1969, pp. 206-09.

"Greek Paragraphs," *Travel and Camera*, May, 1969, pp. 46, 51.

"The White Rose," *Ladies' Home Journal*, July, 1971, pp. 96-97, 127-28. [About his meeting with Colette]

"Portrait of Myself," *Cosmopolitan*, July, 1972, pp. 130-34.

"We'd Get Along Without You Very Well," *Esquire*, June, 1974, p. 114.

"An Interview with Myself," *Daily Telegraph Magazine* (London), July 12, 1974, pp. 29-30.

"Elizabeth Taylor," *Ladies' Home Journal*, December, 1974, pp. 72, 76, 78, 151.

"Mojave," *Esquire*, June, 1975, cover page, pp. 83-91; "La Côte Basque, 1965," *Esquire*, November, 1975, pp. 110-18, 158; "Unspoiled Monsters," *Esquire*, May, 1976, pp. 55-68, 122-35; "Kate McCloud," *Esquire*, December, 1976, pp. 82-96. [All of these are excerpts from an autobiographical novel in progress, "Answered Prayers."]

Note: in 1979, Capote began contributing to Andy Warhol's magazine *Interview*, a series of "Conversational Portraits." Early subjects include Capote's visits with cleaning lady Mary Sanchez, dermatologist Norman Orentreich, the late Human Rights commissioner Robert Livingston, and Marilyn Monroe. (See Arthur Bell, "A Conversation with Capote," *Village Voice*, August 8, 1979, pp. 32-33.)

SECONDARY SOURCES

FLEMING, ANNE TAYLOR. "The Private World of Truman Capote." *New York Times Magazine*, July 9, 1978, pp. 22-25; July 16, 1978, pp. 12-13, 15, 44. The best and most recent of the Capote interviews.

HALLOWELL, JOHN W. *Fact and Fiction: The New Journalism and the Nonfiction Novel.* Chapel Hill: University of North Carolina Press, 1977. Devotes considerable attention to *In Cold Blood* as well as to Capote's other exercises in reportage.

HASSAN, IHAB. *Radical Innocence: Studies in the Contemporary American Novel.* Princeton, N.J.: Princeton University Press, 1961, pp. 230-58. The best concise introduction to Capote's use of theme and form.

HILL, PATI. "Truman Capote." *Writers at Work: The Paris Review Interviews.* Ed. Malcolm Cowley. New York: Viking Press, 1960, pp. 283-89. An enlightening interview with Capote that is more reliable than most of its kind.

MALIN, IRVING. *New American Gothic.* Carbondale: Southern Illinois University Press, 1962. Valuable for its exploration into the gothic legacy which Capote shares.

MORRIS, ROBERT K. "Capote's Imagery." In *Truman Capote's "In Cold Blood."* Ed. Irving Malin. Belmont, Cal.: Wadsworth, 1969, pp. 176-86. An accurate and well-documented discussion of Capote's image patterns.

NANCE, WILLIAM L. *The Worlds of Truman Capote.* New York: Stein and Day, 1970. The first full-length treatment of Capote's work, written with the advantage of first-hand interviews.

NEWQUIST, ROY. "Truman Capote." *Counterpoint.* Chicago: Rand-

McNally, 1974, pp. 75-83. Entertaining, if not probing, interview
with the author.

PLIMPTON, GEORGE. "The Story Behind a Nonfiction Novel." *New York
Times Book Review*, January 16, 1966, pp. 2-3. A brief but
informative insight into Capote's attitude toward *In Cold Blood*.
Valuable as a general approach to the author.

RUOFF, GENE W. "Truman Capote: The Novelist as Commodity." In *The
Forties: Fiction, Poetry, Drama*. Ed. Warren French. Deland, Fla.:
Everett/Edwards, 1969, pp. 261-69. One of the better assessments
of Capote's initiation into the world of letters.

Index

Alexander, Shana, 103
Archebald, William, 29
As I Lay Dying (William Faulkner), 26
Ashida, Mrs. 109
Austin, Jane, 131

Baker, Carlos, 26
Bankhead, Tallulah, 32
Baro, Gene, 87
Blake, Robert, 117–18
Bogart, Humphrey, 27
Brando, Marlon, 28, 95, 99–100
Breen, Robert, 97
Breit, Harvey, 27
Brooks, Richard, 117
Buckley, William, 32
Bruce, David K. E., 30
Burke, Tom, 17

Capote, Joseph Garcia, 21
Capote, Truman: biography, 18–33;
  Mystery Writers of America Edgar
  Allan Poe Award, 31; National Institute of Arts and Letters Award, 29;
  O Henry Memorial Award, 25; on
  death, 30; on play writing, 27; on
  short fiction, 34; "party of the decade," 31–32; public life, 15–17, 31;
  reportage, 28, 34, 94–95; schooling,
  18–22; "second career," 28–29

WORKS: PLAYS AND FILMSCRIPTS:
"Among the Paths to Eden" (televi-
  sion play), 31
Beat the Devil, 27
Breakfast at Tiffany's (screen ver-
  sion), 29
Grass Harp, The (play), 26–27, 31
House of Flowers (play), 27, 31

In Cold Blood (screen version), 31,
  95, 117
Innocents, The, 29

WORKS: PROSE
"Among the Paths to Eden," 35, 37,
  46–47, 126
Answered Prayers, 33
Breakfast at Tiffany's, 28–29, 37, 41,
  62, 70–71, 85, 88–93, 123–25,
  127, 129–30
"Children on Their Birthdays," 37,
  59–63, 70, 90, 119, 125–26, 129
"Curious Gift, A," 29
"Diamond Guitar, A," 49, 62–64, 70,
  114, 123–25, 129
"Duke in His Domain, The," 28, 94,
  99–101, 120, 123
" 'Extreme Magic'—An Awake Dream,
  Cruising Up the Yugoslavian
  Coast," 31
"Faulkner Dances," 26
Grass Harp, The, 26, 37, 62, 64,
  70–71, 81–88, 113, 119–20, 122–28,
  130
"Headless Hawk, The," 35, 37, 39–43,
  57, 59, 63, 90, 120, 122, 129
"House in Sicily, A," 26
"House of Flowers," 68–70, 91, 129
In Cold Blood, 29–32, 49, 68, 94, 96,
  101–18, 120, 122–24, 126–28, 130
"Jug of Silver," 37, 57–59, 62–63, 70,
  119, 125, 127
Local Color, 26, 94–97, 101, 120,
  123–25
"Master Misery," 35, 37, 43–46, 49,
  57, 63, 70, 126, 129
"Mink of One's Own, A," 25, 35–38,
  40, 50, 119, 128

143

Index